IRELAND
In Old Photographs

IRELAND
In Old Photographs

Introduction by J.J. Lee
Text by Carey Schofield

Compiled by Sean Sexton

A BULFINCH PRESS BOOK

Little, Brown and Company
Boston · New York · Toronto · London

Photographs copyright © 1994 by Sean Sexton
Text copyright © 1994 by Carey Schofield
Introduction copyright © 1994 by J.J. Lee

Produced by Calmann & King Ltd

frontispiece A river fisherman and his coracle, Ireland's traditional design of small boat.
Unknown, 1860s. Albumen print.

First North American Edition

ISBN 0-8212-2128-0

Library of Congress Catalog Card Number 94-75736

Bulfinch Press is an imprint and trademark of Little, Brown and Company (Inc.)
Published simultaneously in Canada by Little, Brown & Company (Canada) Limited

PRINTED IN SLOVENIA

Sean Sexton would like to thank the very many people and organisations who have helped him. In particular thanks are owed to the following:
In Britain – Edward Chandler for photographic research, Nicholas Burnett for photographic processes, Stewart Johnstone for copying the photographic prints, Dr Murray MacKinnon for photographic consultancy, the Photo Factory, Aberdeen, Andy Cowan, David Koos, Daniella Dangoor, John Benjafield, Beryl Vosburgh, Janette Rosing, Zelda Cheadle, Peter Ryde, Eamonn Nolan, Edward Power, John Young, Peter Agius, Pablo Butcher, Badr El-Hage, Bill Barnes, James Shiels, E. Earle, Kenneth Griffith, Michael Graham-Stewart, David Hooper, Susan Haines, Lady Langham, Lord Gowrie, Ward Lloyd, John Ritchie, Gwyn Nichols, Pyms Gallery, David Allison, Shlomo Breur, Valerie Lloyd, Reubens, John Maldon, Sidney Ray FRPS, Jane McAusland, Lydia Cresswell-Jones, Ian and Angela Moore, Alan and Mary Hobart, India Dhargalkar and Lindsey Stewart of Christies, Phillippe Garner and Clarissa Bruce of Sothebys, Phillips, as well as vital reference material from the catalogues of these auction-houses, the National Army Museum, the Victoria and Albert Museum, Terence Pepper of the National Portrait Gallery, the Public Records Office, the National Maritime Museum, the Imperial War Museum, the British Library, Ian Leith of the Royal Commission for Historical Monuments, John Williams-Davies of the National Museum of Wales, R. Iestyn Hughes of the National Library of Wales.
In Ireland – Pádraig Ó Snodaigh, Professor Thomas P. O'Neill, Lord Rosse, John O'Callaghan, Charles Cooney, Professor Conroy, Neil Kennedy, John Farrell, Seán Ó Lúing, Dr Eilís Ní Dhuibhne, Donal Markham, Dabheoc Rynne, Martin Staunton, Bridget Mary Mahon, Ciaran Caughey, Pádraig Madden, the Irish Architectural Archive Dublin, Royal Society of Antiquaries of Ireland, Dr Noel Kissane of the National Library of Ireland, National Archives Dublin, Luke Dodd of the Famine Museum, Michael McCaughan of the Ulster Folk and Transport Museum, Peter Walshe of the Guinness Museum.
In the United States – Michael Tsangaris, Joe Hengeler, the Lee Gallery in Washington, Professor Eoin McKiernan.
In Germany – Steffen Wolff.

CONTENTS

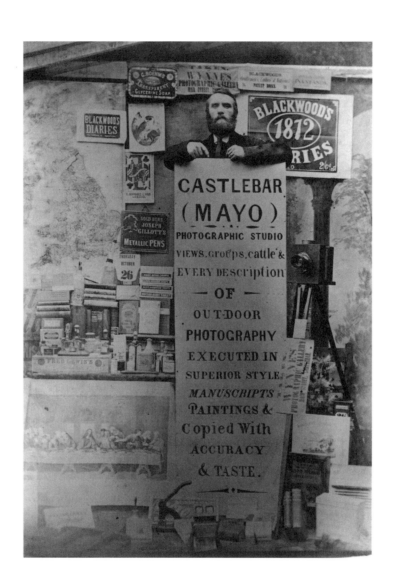

INTRODUCTION

By J.J. Lee

Photography burst on an astonished and excited public with the announcement of Louis Daguerre's invention of his process in Paris in August 1839. Application of the process spread rapidly throughout Europe and America, as the public – or at least the middle and upper classes who could afford the cost – jostled to gaze on their own images, as well as on congenial scenes of people and places. A market quickly emerged among the more comfortable classes in Ireland, and the first commercial studio opened in the Rotunda, in the centre of Dublin, in October 1841. Although surviving photographic scenes from the 1840s are extremely sparse, the numbers grow throughout the 1850s, and by the end of the century that early trickle has become a flood. Sean Sexton's patiently and sensitively accumulated collection adds significantly to the pictorial history of the period it covers.

That century was a most eventful one in Irish history. The Great Famine of 1845-50, in which probably a million people died, and from which another million fled as emigrants, whether across the Irish Sea, or across the Atlantic, still lay in the future when Daguerre made his discovery. Ireland then had a population of more than eight million, which placed it among the most populous states in Europe at that time. A century later, the country, North and South, had only four and one half million inhabitants. Uniquely among countries of the world, its population had fallen, indeed nearly halved, over the intervening century. Half of that loss had, it is true, occurred in the Famine years themselves. But the population continued to decline inexorably in the following century. The country lost another two million people between 1850 and 1920. Ironically enough, population decline coincided with political and, in some respects, social resurgence. After generations punctuated by political unrest, reflected in the Young Ireland rising in 1848, the Fenian rising of 1867, the Land War which erupted in 1879, and continued spasmodically during the following decade, and the Easter Rising of 1916, Ireland finally achieved at least a version of sovereignty in 1921, following the War of Independence that began in 1919. Statehood was achieved at the expense of partition so that two parliaments existed on Irish soil in 1930 where none had existed a century before. Political upheaval was paralleled, at least in certain respects, by social upheaval. Where the landlord class dominated property relations in 1840, it had vanished as the lord of the earth a century later. Indeed, its back was broken within a half century of its apparent invincibility on the eve of the Famine. The period whose images are recorded in this collection was one of dramatic, and often turbulent, change.

The various phases in the history of the time can be detected in the changing emphasis of the collection. The Daguerreotype process was initially very expensive. Only the upper and middle classes could afford the cost involved, not only as consumers, but as producers also. A lot of time and money was required. Denizens of 'the big houses', as the homes of the landed classes were popularly known, had these resources disproportionately at their disposal. The early years of photography accordingly tended to be par excellence a gentry activity. Francis Edmund Currey, agent to the Duke of Devonshire at Lismore Castle in Waterford, can be

left The photographer Thomas Wynne
poses for a colleague inside his studio at his shop in the Main Street of Castlebar.
Unknown, October 1871. Albumen print.

above left Francis Edmund Currey. The pioneer
photographer was the Duke of Devonshire's land
agent at Lismore Castle in County Waterford. The
agent on such an estate was a person of some
standing in the neighbourhood, with the time and
the money necessary to pursue a hobby such as
photography. Currey's work reveals a keen interest
in the countryside and its people, as well as in the
technical aspects of photography. The Duke of
Devonshire's tenants were treated well during the
famine, with many having their rents halved during
the famine of 1845-49, and it is reasonable to pre-
sume that Currey, as the land agent, had some
influence over this policy. Currey is also known to
have been even-handed in his treatment of
Protestants and Catholics on the estate and it is

arguable that such sympathetic attitudes can be
seen in his photography.
Mr Kilburn, 234 Regent Street, London, c.1850.
Hand-coloured daguerreotype.

above right The photographer Lady Augusta
Crofton, with her sliding box wet plate camera, a
present from her father from the Great Exhibition
of 1851. Augusta Crofton married, in 1866, Luke
Dillon (later Lord Clonbrock). Several members of
both the Dillon and Crofton families are known to
have been enthusiastic photographers.
From a Crofton family album, c.1860. Gold-toned
albumen print.

considered representative of this type. His scenes of people and places around Lismore in the early 1850s constitute a valuable part of this collection.

Photography was one of the relatively few public activities that could be pursued by ladies as well as gentlemen. Once again, the ladies of the landed classes were well to the fore. Mary, Countess of Rosse, made Birr Castle a centre of photographic activity, and became one of the first women to join the Dublin Photographic Society in 1856. Lady Augusta Crofton became even better known. She made the Clonbrock House collection in County Galway one of the finest in the country from the 1860s. Of course, what the gentry wished to record was often what they wanted the world to see, not things as they really were. Every photograph has its own history – the history of the photographer no less than the history of the sitter or of the scene.

The prominence with which officers and soldiers feature in the early years reminds us how central a role the military played in the life of Anglo-Ireland. Many a gentry family had a son in the forces, if not in Ireland itself, then somewhere in the empire. Irishmen also made up a disproportionate segment of the rank and file, not only in the Irish regiments specifically recruiting in Ireland, but in other units as well. Army officers, too, feature prominently among the early photographers. They had time on their hands and the raw material immediately available in the barracks. The British army was much more prominent in the life of 'Society' than the Irish army has ever been. The Irish army has been the army of the people, and fits naturally into the life of the country. The British army in Ireland was the army of a caste, and the mentality of that caste was bound to be more ingrained when the authority of the ruling class derived, in the last resort, from its command of the formal forces of violence.

Of course this was to some extent the role of the army in many European countries, even self-governing ones. It was not only a force for protection against external aggression – when it was not engaged in external aggression itself – but also offered protection against internal unrest. Few European countries were deeply imbued with the democratic spirit, much less democratic electoral systems, in the mid nineteenth century. The army in Victorian Ireland could not conceivably be required for protection against external aggression. Nor was it in a position to launch aggression itself. Its role was to guard against unruly subjects. It was the long stop, in cricketing parlance, the defender of last resort against political subversion.

Political subversion could, in Irish circumstances, express itself in social instability. The army could at least be put on standby, even if it was not itself directly involved, at the scenes of evictions. Some of the most striking scenes in the Sexton collection relate to evictions – the well-known Vandeleur ones in Clare in 1888, and the less familiar, but equally harrowing episodes, at Falcarragh in Donegal, in the same year.

We owe these scenes partly to progress in the art of photography itself. The discovery of the dry plate process by Richard Leach Maddox in 1878 allowed photographers to travel light, unencumbered by transportable darkrooms. Evictions in remote west of Ireland areas could now be brought to the attention of a wider public reasonably cheaply. Nevertheless, that wider public still remained largely middle-class. The Manchester firm responsible for the Falcarragh photographic project advertised its pictures at prices that were well beyond the pockets of the victims.

Photographs had, it is true, become much cheaper since the 1850s. A single normal sized portrait then cost about £2, or more than double the average working man's weekly wage. Prices fell sharply from the 1860s, following André Disderi's discovery of 'how to take several negatives on the one glass plate and develop and print them as one'. Nevertheless, the forty shillings (£2) demanded by Robert Banks, the Manchester photographer of the Falcarragh evictions, for a complete set of thirty photographs mounted in a scrap album, would still have

The Right Honourable Otho Fitzgerald MP,
founder member and first chairman of the Dublin Photographic Society.
William Lawrence, Dublin, c.1864. Albumen print.

been well beyond the pockets of the poorer orders, or even of the lower middle classes. Even one shilling (5 pence) for a cabinet photograph would have been a luxury for many a family, and that was the cheapest on offer. Their intended market must have been mainly urban, and possibly even more among liberal supporters of Gladstone's Home Rule policy in Britain than in Ireland itself.

Certainly, the turf (peat) cutters and turf carriers who feature in several photographs are unlikely to have provided a market. It is good to be reminded of the important role of turf in the rural economy. It is useful, too, to have so graphically illustrated the fact that much of the literally back-breaking work of the carrying of the creels of turf from the bogs was done by the women, at least in families that could not afford even a donkey, or on land where even a donkey could not find a footing. Photographs here remind us of the role of the donkey in the economy of the poor. The donkey was a much maligned, and sadly, much abused animal, which, however despised by the more supercilious observers, constituted crucial wealth for the smallholder, and a blessed deliverance from dreadful drudgery for many a woman.

Women feature prominently also in the market scenes that recur throughout the collection. The viewer here will sense the central role of fish markets, potato markets, and street markets in general at a time when, before refrigeration or even elementary storage facilities in many houses, housewives in town had to buy fresh food on a daily basis. Traditional emphasis by academic historians on 'high' finance and the glamour of export markets, dominated by male entrepreneurs, diverts our attention from the central role of women in the humbler retail markets at home. Humble such markets may have been, but they were absolutely essential to the welfare of the family.

The collection nicely blends urban with rural scenes. The photographs of urban Ireland remind us of some familiar Dublin landmarks, as well as drawing our attention to less familiar ones, like the Claddagh in Galway. Housing conditions in the Claddagh can be traced in a series of photographs stretching from the thatched cottages of the 1860s down to the 1930s, when these cottages were just beginning to be demolished in favour of new, slated, two-storey houses in the slum clearance drive of Mr de Valera's *Fianna Fail* government – sometimes, apparently, much to the disgruntlement of the oldest inhabitants.

Maritime history, a much neglected feature of Irish history, is well represented in the quay scenes from Cork, Dublin and other ports and fishing villages, recalling the role of the ship in the life of an island people, both in the day-to-day economy and as the vehicle of emigration and trade.

The collection also contains many fine portraits of public figures of varied political persuasions. These include Fenians like James Stephens and Charles Kickham, British government figures like Charles Trevelyan, outstanding public leaders like Parnell and Davitt later in the century, and renowned nationalists like de Valera and Collins in more modern times. Completing the political portrait there are sobering scenes from the War of Independence of 1919-21, and from the even more poignant Civil War of 1922-3.

There were of course other traditions in Ireland as well. A number of British public figures had their Irish admirers. The Prince and Princess of Wales visited various Dublin exhibitions, and even ventured to what they would have deemed the exotic wilds of Connemara. Royalty always had a market in Ireland under the Union, whether among the politically loyal or the socially deferential. Most of the landlord class, and some of the middle class, not only the Protestant middle class, but the 'Castle Catholic' element, remained staunchly Unionist into the twentieth century. Photographers were not backward in satisfying their demand for suitable scenes and portraits.

One of the strengths of the collection is that it does not concentrate exclusively on the South. There are photographs of the famous Harland and Wolff shipyard, and of an Orange Parade in 1888. Perhaps the most memorable is the photograph of an Ulster Volunteer Force group in 1914, presumably equipped with the fruits of the Larne gun running in April 1914, when Ulster Unionists landed 25,000 rifles from Germany to defend themselves against the threat of imminent home rule being imposed by Herbert Asquith's Liberal Government. Images like these remind us of the existence of a vigorous popular Unionist political culture in the North of Ireland.

This collection then provides a visual record – naturally selective, but extraordinarily illuminating – of the social and political life of Ireland that deepens our perceptions of its people and places. Readers will have their own favourites. My own would include the picture of the anonymous labourer of 1853, and the piper Turlogh McSweeney from 1911. These are portraits of the poor, of the marginal men in society. Yet they convey a sense of extraordinary dignity, of self-respect, which somehow reminds us of the innate value of every individual, however humble they may be.

Sean Sexton's splendid collection brings vividly to life scenes, familiar and unfamiliar, which enable us to empathise with the earlier generations who have trodden the same ground as ourselves, and whose likenesses are so evocatively preserved.

Chapter One

EARLY PHOTOGRAPHY IN IRELAND

Photographs were first taken in Ireland around 1840, very shortly after Monsieur Daguerre invented the process that bore his name. The daguerreotype process produced a very highly defined image but its great disadvantage was that the original could not be copied. An Englishman, William Henry Fox Talbot, who had been working on the same problem for some years, quickly registered the patent for his own invention. Fox Talbot's method used very thin sheets of paper, coated with salts. When the photograph was removed, a negative was left behind which could be printed repeatedly. The quality of the image was poorer than with Daguerre's method, and exposure times were longer, but the ability to reproduce the picture more than outweighed these considerations. So although the first photographic studios to appear in Dublin advertised daguerreotypes, they also sometimes used Fox Talbot's methods. These studios specialised in portraits of individuals or of families, but they also photographed city scenes and landscapes. The invention of the wet collodion process in 1851 shortened exposure times from several minutes to a few seconds, and the glass negative produced could be used to make an unlimited number of high-quality prints. Preparing and sensitising the glass plates was a time-consuming procedure, although the photographs were advertised as 'instantaneous', but the quick exposures and the immediate development of the images meant that the photographer knew within a few minutes whether or not the results were satisfactory. Stereoscopic pictures, small twin images taken with a double-lensed camera, viewed through a 'stereoscope' to give an impression of depth to the scene, were mostly taken by the wet collodion process, and became tremendously fashionable during the 1850s and 1860s. The next major development came in the 1870s, with the discovery that combining gelatine with other chemicals on glass produced a practicable dry rather than wet plate. At last, photographers were able to move around relatively freely, without needing to haul vast quantities of equipment around with them; and there was no need to rush to develop the dry-plates. All the photographer needed to carry with him was his camera, tripod and stock of glass-plates.

The possibilities of photographic journalism do not seem to have been realised in the early days. No photographs of the terrible Irish Potato Famine (1845-49) are known to exist, for example, although genuine images of the suffering would have been invaluable to those who were attempting to awaken the public conscience, in Ireland as well as in England and elsewhere. Presumably the physical difficulties of transporting bulky photographic and developing equipment account for the slow development of photographic reporting, rather than sheer lack of imagination.

During the 1850s the gentry and aristocracy began to take up photography as a recreation. Women of these classes, in particular, made a notable contribution to early Irish photography, no doubt partly because their opportunities in other fields were so limited. Augusta Crofton and Louisa Warenne were particularly gifted nineteenth-century photographers, but they were by no means the only women recording what they saw around them. Inevitably,

left Portrait of two young girls.
John Gregory Crace, c.1853. Gold-toned salted paper print.

A gateway at Lismore Castle.
Francis Edmund Currey, c.1853. Salted paper print.

they tended to photograph their own circle, rather than portraying society as a whole, but they are remarkable not only for their technical expertise, but for the intelligence and for the aesthetic judgement they brought to their craft.

At the same time, commercial studios were springing up in Dublin and other major Irish towns. By 1865 there were 24 photographers' studios in Grafton Street, Westmoreland Street and Sackville Street, the capital's smartest shopping district. These studios specialised in portraits, and advertised a great variety of techniques, to lure their clientele to repeated sittings. There were different sizes, from *cartes de visite* 2¾ by 3⅝ of an inch (70mm by 93mm) to life-size, and there was every conceivable type of frame and case. There were '*Cartes Siamoises*', two pictures of the same person in a double frame, and there were 'diamond cameos', four images of the subject in one sitting. Every studio also employed teams of colourists, often former painters, who would tint images delicately in watercolour or mezzotint, or smother them in oil paint. The studios also began sending their photographers out to take pictures of the country's most famous beauty spots and attractive townscapes; by the 1890s they had covered most of Ireland. Such photographs appealed to the growing number of people travelling for recreation, and by the turn of the century the studios had begun to publish postcards. Some of the country's most distinguished photographers were employed by the big studios, including Robert French, who had been a member of the Royal Irish Constabulary before going to work for William Lawrence, who was probably the most successful of the Dublin proprietors.

From the earliest days of photography there was the possibility of falsification. The medium invited its practitioners to improve upon reality, and this they frequently chose to do. Not only were portraits devised to flatter clients, but scenes of country people, especially, were often arranged to incorporate the quaintness that the sentimental bourgeoisie liked to associate with rural life. Pictures might be blatantly fabricated, with friends of the photographer dressed up as happy peasants living an idyllic existence, or they might involve real country people posed in such a way as to pander to middle-class taste. These lies of the camera are harder to detect, and in many cases it is impossible now to be certain whether or not an image is wholly authentic. Photographs of the middle and upper classes are also frequently contrived, partly to improve the image aesthetically, and partly as a result of the limitations imposed by photographic techniques of the time.

left Group portrait. The identity of the sitters is not known but the picture is believed to have been taken in the photographic studio of the Duke of Devonshire's Lismore Castle. The sitters may have been tenants on that estate.
John Gregory Crace, 1853. Albumen print.

above An Irish labourer. Ambrotype portrait photographs of the working classes dressed in working clothes are rare.
Unknown, 1850s. Quarter plate ambrotype, wet collodion positive on glass.

EARLY PHOTOGRAPHY IN IRELAND

above Ambrotype of three unidentified sitters. The woman on the right also appears at right in the illustration on page 22.
Anonymous, c.1860. Hand tinted, wet collodion positive on glass.

above right Head Constable Kieley and the egg woman. Documentary photography was rare,

anywhere in the world, at this date. The old woman, selling surplus farm produce from door to door or at local markets, is gazing at the camera with wonderment; it is probably the first time that she has seen such a contraption.
Francis Edmund Currey, c.1853. Salted paper print.

bottom right Portrait of a lady, Miss Passy.
Francis Edmund Currey, 1854. Salted paper print.

EARLY PHOTOGRAPHY IN IRELAND

A very early landscape taken at Donemark near
Bantry, County Cork.
Attributed to Hugh Owen, early 1850s.
Salted paper print.

The original photographer's caption reads, 'Taken
on the morning of the day after the Bridge of
Lismore was carried away by the flood of
November 2nd, 1853.' An early and rare
documentary photograph.
Francis Edmund Currey, 1853. Albumen print.

above Group portrait. The young woman seated in the middle is probably Suzy Crofton. The image is also unusual for this process as having been made outdoors.
Circle of Augusta Crofton, c.1857. Wet collodion positive on glass.

top right Suzy Crofton.
Circle of Augusta Crofton, c.1853. Hand-coloured daguerreotype.

bottom right The Baldwin sisters, with mesmerised expressions presumably arising from the need for stillness during the long exposure time.
John Gregory Crace, c.1853. Salted paper print.

EARLY PHOTOGRAPHY IN IRELAND

above 'The Death of Chatterton', after Wallis's painting of the same name. Piracy of famous images seemed particularly common amongst Dublin photographers. In this case, the photographer James Robinson viewed the painting in Grafton Street and returned to his studio to construct a similar set, employing his apprentice to stand in for the dying poet. The photograph was advertised in several Dublin papers and resulted in a court action banning the exhibition and sale of the image. *James Robinson*, 1859. Albumen print.

right The Old Weir Bridge, Killarney. *Payne Jennings*, 1860s. Albumen print.

EARLY PHOTOGRAPHY IN IRELAND

above A young boy in a sailor suit poses appropriately, but none too happily, with a model naval cannon.
Attributed to Augusta Crofton (from an album compiled by Lady Bandon), c.1865. Gold-toned albumen print.

top right Ship at Galway. Ships and harbours were favourite subjects for nineteenth-century photographers, both for the romantic imagery they offered of the possibility of escape and adventure, and as technical masterpieces.
Attributed to Augustavus Darcy, c.1863. Albumen print.

bottom right Dungarvan Harbour, County Waterford. This was mainly a fishing harbour, but in the decade before this photograph was taken men and women had set sail in their thousands from the larger Irish ports, bound for America or for Britain, in the hope of a better life. In September 1846 there had been a riot involving troops and fatalities in Dungarvan when a crowd tried to prevent food exports during the famine.
Francis Edmund Currey, 1854. Albumen print .

EARLY PHOTOGRAPHY IN IRELAND

27

EARLY PHOTOGRAPHY IN IRELAND

top left 'The Spout', a well and drinking trough on the Lismore estate. Here, Currey is not only recording a scene from everyday rural life, he is also experimenting with light and shade.
Francis Edmund Currey, c.1855. Albumen print.

bottom left Milkmaids. Idyllic rural scenes were frequently posed, as this seems to be, with the photographer's family and friends dressing up as idealised country people. This is an example of an image where the photographer has had a clear artistic intention beyond simple reportage.
Dr William Despard Hemphill, 1857. Gold-toned albumen print.

above 'Lady Blessington's Bath', a well-known boating pool in County Tipperary. Note the British Union Flag on the boat.
Dr William Despard Hemphill, c.1865. Albumen print from a wet plate negative.

EARLY PHOTOGRAPHY IN IRELAND

top left Portrait of a young woman.
Lord Otho Fitzgerald, 1855. Salted paper print.

bottom left Lady Cloncurry and an unidentified
young girl, possibly a daughter or other young
relative.
Unknown, 1866. Albumen print.

above Group portrait of young men about town.
Again, the long exposure time has led to fixed
expressions.
Robinson, Dublin, c.1858. Hand-tinted wet collodion
positive on glass.

EARLY PHOTOGRAPHY IN IRELAND

'Summer Scene On The Middle Lake Killarney',
as described in the original photographer's caption.
Payne Jennings, 1860s. Albumen print.

Chapter Two

THE ADMINISTRATION

'Ireland is like a ship on fire, it must be extinguished or cut adrift.' So William Pitt the Younger justified the Act of Union (1801), which swept away Dublin's Parliament. The Act represented one of the great tragedies in Irish history, but like many of England's fatal mistakes in Ireland it was at least partly motivated by muddled goodwill. It had been precipitated by the rising of 1798, which many at Westminster interpreted as evidence that Protestant Ascendancy rule was unacceptable to the largely Catholic population. So Ireland was to be united to Britain, and it was intended that Catholic Emancipation would follow. From the English point of view the Act of Union was an enlightened and benevolent piece of legislation, which would placate Ireland and enable England to concentrate on the war with Revolutionary France. French help for the Irish rebellion in 1798 had highlighted the risk that Ireland might be used as the base for an attack on England.

But the 1798 rising had not, in fact, been a Catholic rebellion. Although it was to degenerate into an orgy of sectarian violence, its leaders had included many Protestants, notably the Dublin lawyer Theobald Wolfe Tone. The abolition of the College Green Parliament, which only eight years earlier had won the right to legislate for Ireland directly, was a catastrophic blow for Irish aspirations to nationhood. Not only was the island reduced to the status of a province, but it was clear that Ireland's own ruling class had betrayed her. Support for the Act of Union was blatantly bought: over fifty Irish parliamentarians were given peerages (or better peerages than the ones they had), and £1,250,000 was spent on bribes. Many among the Ascendancy (the Protestant ruling class) convinced themselves that Union guaranteed their protection, although it simultaneously undermined their identity.

Twenty-eight peers, four bishops, and one hundred MPs represented Ireland in the new Parliament of Great Britain and Ireland at Westminster. Catholic Emancipation did not follow the Act of Union: George III refused his assent to the measure, insisting that it conflicted with his Coronation Oath to defend Protestantism. The Act of Union did not even succeed in pacifying Ireland. Barely two years after the Act was passed a rising was led by a young Dubliner by the name of Robert Emmet, who had spent an inheritance on building up arms caches in the city. Emmet succeeded only in involving a mob of fifty or sixty of Dublin's wretched slum-dwellers in this entirely futile affair. He is supposed to have impressed those who saw him in the dock, after he was condemned to death. 'Let no man write my epitaph', he is said to have insisted. 'When my country takes her place among the nations of the earth, ... let my epitaph be written.'

The Act of Union effectively deepened the sectarian divide in Irish life. All sorts and conditions of Protestants existed in Ireland, from the wealthy landowners to the gentry, prosperous farmers and tenants scraping to survive, and Dublin professionals and tradespeople, but with notable exceptions they tended to support the Union, and they were certainly seen by the

left Mr Gillies, a pioneer of the Grenadier Guards.
Note the metal stand, behind the subject's head, holding him steady.
He might have had to stand perfectly still for a minute or more
for this photograph to be taken.
Sir Robert Shaw, Dublin, 1857. Albumen print.

Lord John Russell (1792-1878),
was British Prime Minister from 1846-52,
during the period of the famine.
Mayall Studio, Regent Street, London, c.1864. Albumen print.

bulk of the Catholic population as doing so. The Catholic Church, having been let down over the question of Emancipation, threw its weight behind Daniel O'Connell, a campaigning lawyer who came to be known as 'the Liberator'.

O'Connell had witnessed some of the violence of the French Revolution, and was committed to constitutional rather than military action. 'No political change whatsoever is worth the shedding of a single drop of human blood', O'Connell asserted. In 1823 he founded the 'Catholic Association', which soon had branches all over Ireland. Members each paid one penny a month subscription, which was collected by priests after Mass. The movement was soon taking £2,000 a week. O'Connell was becoming a force to be reckoned with in Ireland. In 1828 he was elected MP for County Clare, although, as a Catholic, he was forbidden to take his seat at Westminster. The Duke of Wellington, then British Prime Minister, was so alarmed at the prospect of another Irish rebellion that he pushed Catholic Emancipation through the British parliament the following year. George IV had succeeded his father in 1820, and although he too resisted Catholic Emancipation, he agreed to it when both Wellington and Sir Robert Peel (earlier derided by O'Connell as 'Orange Peel' for his opposition to Emancipation) told him that they would otherwise resign. Emancipation entitled Catholics in Britain, as well as in Ireland, to enter public life, and its achievement was largely due to the efforts of Daniel O'Connell.

However, O'Connell's subsequent campaign, for the repeal of the Act of Union, was doomed to failure. Irish Protestant opposition was effectively mobilised, and faced with what

Sir Charles Trevelyan (1807-86). As Chief Secretary to the Treasury
Trevelyan administered, seemingly with a clear conscience,
such inadequate relief works as were attempted during the famine.
Southwell, London, c.1860. Albumen print.

The Times called 'monster meetings', at which hundreds of thousands-strong crowds listened to the Liberator's impassioned speeches at historic sites, the British Government itself came to see O'Connell's 'Repeal Association' as potentially dangerous. A meeting was planned for Sunday, October 8th, 1843, at Clontarf and troops were lined up along the approaches to the meeting-place. The stage looked set for a massacre, but O'Connell and his lieutenants succeeded in persuading the gathering crowds to go home. Nevertheless, he was imprisoned for three months, and after his release he recognised that the Repeal campaign was hopeless. O'Connell's style of campaigning, of raising mass support but restricting himself to constitutional methods, was to act as a model for the Irish Home Rule Party of the later nineteenth century. But the peasantry, upon whom O'Connell had relied, were to be fatally weakened by starvation and emigration in the middle decades of the century.

Amid the periodic upheavals of rebellion and political agitation, the Dublin Castle administration continued to function. The Lord Lieutenant, or Viceroy, was the monarch's representative in Ireland, officially responsible for the civilian government and for the armed forces. He also maintained a Court at Dublin Castle, and presided over the social life of the city. But his position was largely ceremonial. After the Act of Union real power lay with the Chief Secretary to the Lord Lieutenant, who was the effective head of the Irish executive. During the nineteenth century the powers of the Chief Secretary's office were extended considerably, until it controlled virtually the entire machinery of government, often to the exasperation of the Lords Lieutenant. Despite the breadth of his power in Ireland, as a member of the British Government and usually a Cabinet Minister, the Chief Secretary tended to spend most of the year at Westminster, leaving his Under-Secretary administratively in charge in Dublin.

From the humanitarian point of view, the great test of the administration during the nineteenth century came with the Famine of the 1840s. Ireland's poorest (one third of the population) had traditionally survived on a diet of potatoes and milk. So, when the potato crop was riddled with blight in the years 1845-49, poverty-stricken families faced starvation, even although food was still being exported from Ireland for sale elsewhere. European political thinking of the time generally favoured a *laissez-faire* approach, believing that market forces ultimately provided the best relief from hardship. However, the initial response of Sir Robert Peel's Conservative government to the crisis, in the autumn of 1845, was to send immediate help. £100,000-worth of wheat from India was distributed, and Peel set about repealing the Corn Laws (which protected British and Irish farmers against imports), in order to lower the price of grain. He authorised public works schemes to provide Irishmen with jobs and hence a source of income, he encouraged charities to help, and he established food depots to make food available to people directly, avoiding traders who might raise their prices at a time of shortage. These measures were successful. No one died of starvation alone that first winter of the famine.

But the next year the potato crop failed entirely and the government in Westminster was faced with a major disaster. The new Liberal Prime Minister, Lord John Russell, led a minority government and was committed to free trade. 'It must be thoroughly understood that we cannot feed the people.' Relief for Irish suffering would have to come from Ireland, and food could not be sold below market price. He allowed charities to distribute free soup, but ordered that public works programmes should be placed under the control of the Board of Works,

THE ADMINISTRATION

left Colonel Dyson, Third Royal Dragoon Guards,
in civilian dress. Note that the same studio table has
been used as in the illustration on page 45.
Sir Robert Shaw, Dublin, 1857. Albumen print.

above Edward VII with local people in Connemara.
The Irish have always insisted that it was a woman
in the Curragh who made a man of Edward, when,
as Prince of Wales, he visited Ireland in 1861.
Chancellor, 1904. Gelatine silver developing out
paper, enlargement.

where bureaucratic delays slowed down the process disastrously. Families wandered the countryside, trying to feed themselves on berries, nettles and grass. By the end of 1846 even in the workhouses people were dying. At this time government depots were opened, and grain was offered for sale to the starving at the market price, plus five per cent. In 1847 epidemics of typhus, dysentery and other diseases spread rapidly among a population already fatally weakened by malnutrition. That year the potato crop was not blighted, and American wheat appeared in Europe, lowering the price. But the government cut back further on relief work, leaving thousands too poor to buy food. In 1848-49 the potato crop failed again. Between 1841 and 1851 one and a half million Irish men, women and children died. Another million emigrated, many of them to America. The population of Ireland was reduced by one fifth: it has never recovered its 1841 figure of just over eight million. Most European administrations of the time would have reacted instinctively to the famine in more or less the same way as the government in Westminster and the authorities in Ireland. But the failure to comprehend the scale of the human misery, and the callousness with which reports of it were received are remarkable, even by the brutal standards of the nineteenth century.

Whereas the Famine displayed the moral bankruptcy of officialdom, it showed the humanity and generosity of individuals. Some landlords reduced rents to help their tenants, and offered food and medical shelter to destitute peasants. The Society of Friends (the Quakers) made the most significant contribution to relief efforts, (£505,000 was raised in Britain and America) far exceeding anything attempted by the Established Church. The British Relief Association contributed £400,000, including a personal donation of £2,000 from Queen Victoria (although she had supported Lord John Russell's tough stance). Three million people were being fed by private charities in the summer of 1847.

The British army represented a major force in the life of Ireland, and thousands of Irishmen served either as soldiers or officers: proportionally twice as many men joined up as in England, Scotland or Wales. The army was glad to have them: Macaulay described Ireland as 'an inexhaustible nursery of the finest soldiers'. Evidently the 'Forces of the Crown' were used to suppress nationalist rebellions, but they do not seem to have been generally viewed as an oppressive foreign army, largely because so many in the ranks were themselves Irish. The armies that defeated Napoleon and planted the British flag in every quarter of the globe included large Irish contingents. Agricultural workers or servants were often recruited into the Army, attracted by regular and relatively good pay (traditionally one shilling a day) and seemingly generous conditions. The urban poor, with their health increasingly undermined by appalling living conditions and less inclined to accept discipline, provided less promising material for the regiments. After fourteen years in the Army a soldier could retire with £21 and a pension for life, and most Regiments would attempt to find jobs for men who had served them well. The police and other employers also reserved positions for former soldiers, and various charities existed to look after those who fell on hard times, or their widows and children. This was at a time when concern for the welfare of employees and tenants was not widespread in Britain. For many, military service was not a bad alternative to emigration.

Vice-Regal Lodge, Dublin. The Lord Lieutenant,
or Viceroy, was the monarch's representative
in Ireland, theoretically presiding over the
administration of the country. In practice, the
position was largely ceremonial, and real power
lay with the Chief Secretary, who was a member
of Parliament in London and sometimes a member
of the Cabinet. The Viceroy's offices were in
Dublin Castle; Vice-Regal Lodge in Phoenix Park
was his official residence. Lord Abercorn, the
Viceroy at this time, is seventh from right in the
back row (bearded, facing camera).
Unknown, 1865. Albumen print.

Dublin Docks and the Customs House. The dome supported a statue of Hope resting on her anchor, with the figures of Britannia and Hibernia embracing each other over the portico.
Payne Jennings, 1860s. Gold-toned albumen print.

THE ADMINISTRATION

top left Captain Lamb and Captain Blinkthorn.
An unusually informal army photograph for its
time.
Unknown, 1855. Albumen print, with a very thin
coating.

bottom left Tom Goff, military portrait. The sketch at
the top left is part of the original composition and is
hand-mounted on the photograph.
Unknown, 1855. Albumen print, with a very thin
coating.

above Portrait of a military gentleman.
Sir Robert Shaw, Dublin, 1857. Albumen print.

THE ADMINISTRATION

above The fifes and drums of the 3rd Battalion, Grenadier Guards at Beggarsbush Barracks, Dublin. Boys as young as fourteen could enlist in the British army and would usually complete their boy service as drummers and either continue as bandsmen or transfer to the ranks at eighteen. *Unknown*, 1868. Albumen print.

top right Officers of the 1st Battalion, Grenadier Guards at the Curragh, County Kildare. *Unknown*, 1875. Gold-toned albumen print.

bottom right An unidentified cavalry officer and his mount. *Robert French*, 1875. Albumen print.

THE ADMINISTRATION

E battery, Royal Horse Artillery. Newbridge,
County Kildare.
Charleton, Newbridge & Curragh, 1912. Sepia-toned
silver print.

above Sergeant Walls, Grenadier Guards. *Unknown*, 1876. Gold-toned albumen print.

top right Grenadier Guards, tug-of-war champions at the Curragh, 1876. The total weight of the champions was 'one ton, three hundredweight, two and a half pounds'. The lightest of them weighed in at 12 stone 7 pounds (79 kg/175 pounds), the heaviest at 19 stone 4 pounds (122 kg/270 pounds). The first man, on the left, is Sergeant Walls (*see above*).
Unknown, 1876. Gold-toned albumen print.

bottom right Royal Artillery Post. Somewhat dishevelled representatives of Her Majesty's Armed Forces. The men are wearing their unit number on their shoulder-straps, and the young man second from left, holding a dog, is wearing a shoesmith's emblem on his sleeve.
James H. McLean, Dublin, 1895. Albumen print.

THE ADMINISTRATION

Chapter Three

THE LAND

Ireland had been and remained an overwhelmingly rural society until well into the twentieth century. However, during the second half of the nineteenth century the nature of life in the countryside changed profoundly. After the famine of the 1840s many smallholdings were consolidated, and gave way to large-field pasturage. This process was encouraged by market forces and by technological developments, but it brought new hardship for many families, driven to destruction by eviction from their homes. Following decades of unrest a series of Land Laws was implemented between 1870 and 1903, further altering the pattern of land-owning, and dramatically improving living standards for many in rural Ireland. It is from this period that most small, family-owned farms dated. Life remained hard for country people, but they were a tough and self-reliant race, on the whole, who raised large families and took great pride in maintaining their standards of morality and good housekeeping.

There were, of course, considerable variations in the standards of living enjoyed by country people. The economy of the north-eastern counties was more diversified than in the rest of the country, and they were generally more prosperous as a result. Similarly, life in Wexford, Carlow, Wicklow, Kildare, Kilkenny and County Dublin, the fertile counties within easy reach of the capital, was usually relatively easy. In the remoter districts it continued to be difficult to extract a living from rocky land. Fishing communities, especially on the north-west coast, were poor, but their food supply was constant, and they therefore survived the famine better than inland farmers.

Women were the backbone of the community, not only running the household and rearing the children, but usually raising pigs and chickens, and occasionally goats, as well. Carding, dyeing and spinning wool were also considered to be female tasks, and in the remoter areas, where life was usually toughest, sheep-shearing might also fall to the women. In times of hardship, when the men might travel to England or Scotland in search of temporary work, their mothers, wives and daughters would take on all the work on the land. There was no cultural taboo against women undertaking hard physical labour, and they were invariably involved in harvesting crops and cutting and carrying home the turf. But at the same time a woman's status in the eyes of the community (crucially, in the judgement of the older women) depended at least partly upon her housewifely skills. The poorest had few opportunities indeed, but among relatively prosperous country people, the ability to feed the family thriftily, to turn fruits and berries from the orchards and hedgerows into jams and surplus vegetables into pickles for the winter, was highly valued. Knitting, smocking, lace-making and embroidery were skills in which an Irish woman would take great pride, and as well as improving the appearance of her family and of the home, she might be able to sell some of her handwork and raise a little cash.

left Mill worker, Jerpoint, County Kilkenny.
An unusually sensitive and humane portrait of a labourer,
neither patronising nor sentimental.
Note the size of the sack, packed with grain,
that this man is used to lifting.
Attributed to Rev. James Graves (a local Church of Ireland Minister),
c.1860. Albumen print.

THE LAND

But the main task of a wife was to produce children, to help around the place and to provide for parents in old age. Despite the prodigious amount of work that might be got out of a healthy daughter, boys were especially prized. A married woman who had failed to produce a son could not be considered to have been entirely successful in life, no matter what else she might have achieved.

As the nineteenth century progressed, and more of Ireland's country people began to live above the level of meagre subsistence, the usual age of marriage rose steadily. On the eve of the famine it was quite normal for girls to marry at sixteen, boys at seventeen or eighteen. As the Catholic Bishop of Raphoe said in 1835, 'They cannot be worse off than they are'. An earthen and turf cabin could be constructed in a couple of days and if the young couple had nothing but a pot and a couple of stools, they were no worse off than most other families. They would simply attempt to scratch a living out of whatever scrap of land their parents could give them. The experience of the famine, bitten deep into the Irish consciousness, ended this way of life. Land was no longer endlessly subdivided; farms now tended to pass to the eldest son, or occasionally to the youngest, leaving the other children to try to find some sort of employment, or to emigrate. By 1900 the average age of marriage for women was 31, for men 39, and considerable numbers of Irish people of both sexes accepted that they would never marry.

In 1891 the Congested Districts Board was established, in an attempt to improve conditions in the heavily populated, but impoverished, western counties. This well-intentioned enterprise was part of the Conservative policy of 'constructive Unionism', or 'killing Home Rule with kindness'. The three million people living in the Western counties (Donegal, Sligo, Leitrim, Roscommon, Galway, Clare, Limerick, Kerry and Cork) could be divided into two classes – 'the poor and the destitute' – the Board found. So cash was to be injected into the area, to raise living standards and provide employment. Road building schemes were introduced, partly as a relief measure for the labourers who were to work on them, and partly to open the area up, so that, at last, it would be easy to transport any surplus the region might produce to the markets of the rest of Ireland. The Congested Districts Board attempted to improve the efficiency of the fishing industry, building harbours, providing money to buy larger boats than the traditional curraghs, and offering low-interest loans for nets and other equipment. Instructors were sent to train local people in the use of modern techniques and equipment. The Board encouraged the sale of herring, mackerel, lobster and other seafood from the western counties by improving transportation, by teaching curing techniques and by supplying ice to keep freshly-caught fish in good condition until it reached the markets. The fishing industry was the success story of the Congested Districts Board. Its attempts to increase agricultural efficiency (improving livestock, training in crop rotation and the prevention of plant diseases) seem to have had little effect on the farms. Some local industries (lace, tweed, knitwear, carpets) were successfully helped by the Board, but in other cases ineffective marketing hampered what might have been viable enterprises.

The Congested Districts Board was also involved in the redistribution of land. Large estates were bought, sometimes by compulsory purchase, and allocated to small farmers, who were given the chance to run a viable holding. The measure had the effect, however, of breaking up the traditional villages – the *clachans* – where all the cabins of the community huddled together, so that people lived in hourly contact with their neighbours, bound together through gossip, story-telling, shared chores, mutual support, ritual squabbling and bitter quarrels. Instead, the now familiar pattern of the West was established – of families living on remote farms at some distance from their neighbours and the rest of their relations. Isolation and

A farmer and his team at work on the harvest.
F.R.A. McCormick, Dublin, c.1930. Toned gelatine
silver transparency.

loneliness replaced the old intimacy. However, many of the country people welcomed the changes, and not only because they guaranteed their survival. In post-famine Ireland there was a reaction against the old way of life associated with the misery. So the *clachans*, with their teeming humanity sunk in poverty, were despised and the independence of the new homesteads prized.

In the same way, many of the traditional wild foods that generations of Irish people had enjoyed came to be rejected in the second half of the nineteenth century, by those who had been driven to scavenging for them, not as delicacies, but in the desperation of hunger. So fungi, cresses and eels all fell out of favour, only to be rediscovered by later generations. By the same token, the prosperity of a family could virtually be assessed in inverse proportion to the amount of potatoes they ate. While the poorest continued to survive mainly on potatoes and buttermilk, better-off families would enjoy a much more varied diet.

The country year was punctuated by a series of festivals, which the population celebrated with great abandon. Christmas, Shrove Tuesday and Easter were commemorated in Ireland as they were throughout Christendom. Other festivals were specific to Ireland. The feast days of St Patrick and St Bridget, for example, both occurring in early spring, were important dates in the calendar. On St Bridget's Eve, 31 January, rushes were pulled from the ground (never cut) and woven into intricate crosses, which were then hung over the entrance to houses and byres, to prevent evil spirits crossing the threshold. Food and a bed of straw were often left out for the Saint, who was believed to wander the countryside on the eve of her feast. The day itself usually ended with a party and a supper of pancakes, and was sometimes enlivened by 'Biddy Boys', groups of youths wearing straw masks and carrying a straw doll, who went from house to house singing songs in Bridget's honour. They would expect to be treated with presents and refreshments in return. St Patrick's Day, 17 March, provided a welcome interruption in Lent, although it is worth pointing out that it was not traditionally celebrated in Ireland with quite the enthusiasm shown by the Irish diaspora in North America. May Day and Midsummer Eve were always the excuse for great festivals and dances and each was traditionally celebrated with bonfires. Hallowe'en was another great excuse for a party, and the occasion of endless rituals connected with welcoming and placating the spirits of the dead, who were known to be walking abroad that night. This was also the date by which all crops had to be gathered in, all fruits picked, and animals returned from their summer pastures. Local fairs also provided the opportunity for people to gather from afar, and to celebrate the occasion with a drink, some singing, and, of course, a dance. If disreputable enough, such a fair might be described as a 'Donnybrook', after the village near Dublin (now a suburb of the city), where the annual fair was notorious for its debauchery and violence.

above Monastery building on Skellig Michael, a tiny rocky island off the Kerry coast which was a noted centre of the early Celtic church.
Mr Mercer, from *Notes on Irish Architecture* by Lord Dunraven, 1875. Carbon transfer print.

twelfth centuries, and are a distinctively Irish creation. In the background, the round tower, standing some 100 feet (30 metres) high.
Mr Mercer, from *Notes on Irish Architecture* by Lord Dunraven, 1875. Carbon transfer print.

overleaf left Monasterboice. St Buite (died c.520) founded this monastery in County Louth, where two small churches, a round tower, three High Crosses and some early gravestones survive. The South Cross, richly ornamented with figured panels, including the Crucifixion, the Last Judgement and the Murder of Abel, is seen here. High Crosses, of which about 150 have survived the passage of time, the climate, Cromwell's men and lesser vandals, were built between the seventh and

overleaf right Ancient Cross, Kells, County Meath. The monastery at Kells was probably founded around 804 for monks fleeing from Iona, in Scotland, which had been burned by the Vikings. It was at about this time, too, that the greatest treasure of Celtic art, the eighth-century illuminated gospel manuscript known as the *Book of Kells,* was brought here from Iona.
Robert French, 1870s. Gold-toned albumen print.

THE LAND

THE LAND

THE LAND

THE LAND

left Close-up of a round tower, the Belfry
of Disert Aengus.
Mr Mercer, from *Notes on Irish Architecture* by Lord
Dunraven, 1875. Carbon transfer print.

above Ruins on Devenish Island, Lough Erne. The
monastery on the island was founded in the sixth
century.
Robert French, c.1890. Albumen print.

above One of the round towers and a section of the
ruins at Clonmacnoise, County Offaly, one of the
most noted centres of early Irish Christianity,
founded c.545 by St Ciaran.
Robert French, c.1890. Albumen print.

right The round tower at Kilmacduagh, County
Galway. The tower is 112 feet (35 metres) high and
dates from the eleventh or twelfth century. As the
photograph makes clear it leans substantially from
the vertical.
Mr Mercer, from *Notes on Irish Architecture* by Lord
Dunraven, 1875. Carbon transfer print.

THE LAND

THE LAND

An artistically composed view of Colleen Bawn
Caves, Killarney, a noted tourist attraction, even at
the time of the photograph.
Robert French, c.1890. Albumen print.

COLLEEN BAWN CAVES. KILLARNEY. 1089 .W.L

THE LAND

left Gathering wood. Ireland has little of its own, and country people depended on turf or on scraps of wood that they could collect from hedgerows, rather than on expensive bought fuel for cooking. The poorest country people relied on straw, stubble and dried horse and cow dung.

Unknown, from an album compiled by Lady Bandon, c.1860. Albumen print.

above 'The Rose of the Suir', a prize-winning bullock. The number of beef cattle in Ireland doubled in the middle years of the century, as the size of farms increased and transport improved. Despite recurrent famine conditions beef became a valuable export.

J. Pender, Waterford, 1863. Albumen print.

THE LAND

67

Haymaking would begin at dawn and carry on
until dusk and involve men, women and children
to make maximum use of a spell of dry weather. At
the beginning of the nineteenth century women
had been actively engaged in cutting the crops, but
the introduction of the scythe, which needed
greater strength than the old sickle, meant that
women tended to be relegated to the tasks of
collecting, tying and stacking. Many itinerant
labourers helped with all aspects of the harvest, but
the workers here look like relatively prosperous
tenant farmers.

Unknown, from an album compiled by Lady Bandon,
c.1860. Albumen print .

above Farm labourers. The people in this
photograph have survived the famine. The
photographer normally photographed members of
her own class; this is a rare example of her work
dealing with members of the working class. It is
almost certainly posed inasmuch as it is highly
unlikely that the pony and trap belonged to the
people shown.
Attributed to Augusta Crofton, c.1857. Albumen print.

top right Carrying home the turf. As in this case,
women frequently dried, stacked and hauled the
creels (large wickerwork baskets) of turf home; an
average household needed about twelve tons a
year.
Robert Welch, c. 1895. Platinum print.

bottom right Estate workers, Castletownroche,
County Cork. The subjects in this photograph
appear to be real workers, rather than gentry
dressed up, as was frequently the case in genre
scenes of country life. The image is one of a stereo
pair taken with a single lens camera that would
have been moved to make the second image.
*Humphrey Haines, 1858. Gold-toned albumen print,
one of a stereo pair.*

THE LAND

A "HAND MADE TURF" BOG, GRANGE, SLIGO. ROOTS OF TREES IN SITU. R.W. 5210.

A turf bog, Grange, County Sligo. Turf – decayed
layers of the peat bog that covers at least one fifth
of Ireland – was cut and dried during the summer.
The top twelve inches (30 cm) burned badly; but
the deeper, black peat dried hard and burned
almost as well as coal.
Robert Welch, c.1890. Platinum print.

THE LAND

Cutting the turf, Clougher, County Fermanagh.
Backbreaking and repetitive labour, with one in
each pair driving the spade and the other lifting
and throwing the sodden slab of turf aside to dry.
Rose Shaw, c.1895. Gelatine silver developed out
print.

THE LAND

73

Open air Mass at Bunlin Bridge, County Donegal.
From the time of the Protestant Reformation, in
the sixteenth century, until Emancipation in 1829,
Catholics throughout Britain and Ireland suffered
considerable legal disadvantages. The prudent, in
Ireland as in Britain, lapsed into Protestantism.
Despite the penalties, the vast majority of the
native Irish were steadfast in their faith, however,
and as the nineteenth century progressed the
Church became a force to be reckoned with in
Ireland. Weekly Mass was not only a religious
occasion; it was also a social event, and it is evident
that the people in this photograph, most of them
from the poorer classes, have made an effort to
smarten themselves up. The priest can be seen
beside his makeshift altar.
Attributed to A. Ayton, Londonderry, 1867.
Gold-toned albumen print.

DUBLIN SCALON

The eviction of tenants for non-payment of rent on the Vandeleur estate. The battering ram was used both to break in to the house and make it uninhabitable after the eviction. The tenants have placed foliage in the doors and windows to make entry more difficult. Evictions were carried out by the sheriff, bailiffs and 'emergency-men' (labourers engaged for the operation), supported by the police and the army.

Unknown, 1888. Albumen print.

THE LAND

McGrath's house, on the Vandeleur estate, after
eviction. Even the horse looks worn out in this
scene of devastation. People who had been evicted
lived in caves, in ruined buildings, or they moved
back into what was left of their own old homes.
Unknown, 1888. Albumen print.

An evicted family at Glenbeigh.
Francis Guy, Cork, 1888. Albumen print.

Eviction on the Olphert Estate, Falcarragh, County Donegal. The local people had a staunch ally in their parish priest, Father MacFadden, who was arrested at the beginning of 1888 for inciting parishioners to withhold their rents. 'Mr Wybrants Olphert', Fr MacFadden wrote from jail, '... has refused the smallest reduction to his Gweedore tenants, not only this year, but every year for the last eight years, when many of them, almost all of them, were living on charity. I am in grips with him on the question of settling with his poor tenants. He obtained absolute decrees against almost fifty of my people at Lifford the other day... A more wretched and miserable lot of tenants there is not to be found in all Ireland... He... prosecuted and evicted them in 1884. Then charity came to their relief. There will be no charity now.'
Robert Banks, 1888. Gold-toned albumen print.

Group photograph, including Fr MacFadden
(seated front, right) and an English delegation.
Robert Banks, 1888. Albumen print.

An evicted family at Derrybeg,
County Donegal.
Robert French, late 1880s. Albumen print.

Patt Spellecy and family, after being evicted from
their home on the Vandeleur estate, County Clare.
Unknown, 1888. Albumen print.

(ESTATE)

Rose McGinley and Grace McGee. 'Described
as two criminals... aged nine and twelve
respectively (they) were arrested for giving bread to
an evicted man aged seventy five.' (from the
original photographer's caption).
Robert Banks, 1888. Gold-toned albumen print.

After the Bailiff's visit. This time the 'emergency-
men' have done their job well, leaving
uninhabitable ruins of a family's home.
Only the fireplace and chimney have
withstood the assault.
Unknown, c.1888. Albumen print.

Grinding grain in a quern, Inishmurray, County
Sligo. By the turn of the century grain was usually
ground in a central mill, but on this late summer
day Mary Heraghty is doing it herself, with a
quern, a time-consuming but effective Stone-Age
device. Note the little boy on the right, dressed as a
girl, for fear the fairies might carry him off (they
would be unlikely to bother about a female). This
was a common way of protecting precious sons.
Robert Welch, 1900. Platinum print.

THE LAND

87

Leenane, County Galway. Horse-drawn
carts deliver groceries, fuel and other necessities,
while the woman in the foreground washes clothes
in the stream.
Robert French, c.1885. Albumen print.

LEENANE. Co.GALWAY.1448. W.L.

Inhabitants of Achill Island, County Mayo.
Robert French, 1890. Albumen print.

Inhabitants of Aranmore. The original caption
reads 'descendants of the Firbolgs', literally, 'dark
people', a slightly contemptuous term for the
people of this isolated community.
Robert Welch, c.1895. Platinum print.

THE LAND

Relief works, Inverin Hill, County Galway. Road
and wall building and other public works could
offer some employment in hard times.
Unknown, c.1890. Albumen print.

Scattery Island, Kilrush, County Clare. Since depopulated as a result of the poverty common in rural Ireland, Scattery Island is situated a little way upstream from the mouth of the Shannon. Note the thatch on the roofs, pegged down against the bitter Atlantic wind. On the beach, a group of the characteristic west coast curraghs, with their high, pointed bows. A seafarer told the writer J.M. Synge, 'A man who is not afraid of the sea will soon be drownded... But we do be afraid of the sea, and we do only be drownded now and again.'
Robert French, c.1890. Albumen print.

Curing mackerel on the League, Castletownshend,
County Cork.
Louisa Warenne, c.1894. Toned matt gelatine
silver print.

THE LAND

Kate Dickinson. Louisa Warenne was one of the
finest 'artistic' photographers of the late nineteenth
century in Ireland.
Louisa Warenne, c.1893. Brown platinum print.

above Curing mackerel for shipment to America,
the Old Jetty, Killybegs, County Donegal.
Robert Welch, c.1910. Developed out gelatine silver
transparency.

top right Turf from Connemara being brought
over to the Aran Islands.
Christine Chichester, c.1910. Sulphur toned gelatine
silver print on rough textured paper.

bottom right Supplies for the Aran Islands being
unloaded by the local men in their boats.
Christine Chichester, c.1910. Sulphur toned gelatine
silver print on rough textured paper.

THE LAND

96

THE LAND

Wreck of the *Leon XIII*, County Clare. The
Coastguards were unable to launch their boat to
help the crew. Instead, local fishermen went out in
their curraghs, and performed the rescue. A church
was founded at Quilty, home of the rescuers, to
commemorate the event and the ship's bell was
later installed in the church.
Unknown, 1907. Gelatine silver printing out paper.

Fishermen at Renard Point, County Kerry. The 'hooker', a single-masted sailboat usually about 35 feet (11 metres) long, 'black-bellied and brown-sailed', was used for carrying fuel and livestock, as well as for fishing. Earlier, men say, it provided a most effective way of importing French brandy, without bothering the Excise man.
Christine Chichester, c.1910. Gelatine silver printing out paper.

THE LAND

Interior of a cabin. This is clearly the home of a relatively prosperous family: the furniture in the room is solid and plentiful, and glimpsed through the open door is a well-made cupboard. A typical 'crane' is suspended over the hearth, from which various pots and utensils can be hung. Note the 'keeping-holes' built into the wall on either side of the hearth. According to old tradition, the hole on the left of the fire belonged to the housewife, that on the right to her husband. The bed on the left of the room, the 'outshot' bed, was often reserved for a grandparent, who would be kept warm at night by the fire.
Robert Welch, c.1890. Platinum print.

THE LAND

A housewife with her poultry.
Christine Chichester, c.1910. Gelatine silver printing
out paper.

Old lady at Castletownshend, County Cork. The
inscription reads: 'Her face was like a leaf torn
from an old volume... It was a most noble face, a
fortress face, strong and massive and honourable in
ruin...'
Louisa Warenne, c.1894. Platinum print.

Irish hawkers. Not particularly respected in the
countryside, hawkers might nevertheless carry
news or gossip with them as they travelled round.
Unknown, c.1900. One of a stereo pair, toned
gelatine printing out paper.

THE LAND

THE LAND

top left Taking the pigs to market. Pigs made
a vital contribution to the budget of many rural
households, especially those with little land. A
smallholding family might buy a couple of piglets in
the spring, feed them on household scraps, and
sell them in the autumn to raise cash. They were
usually reared by the women of the family.
Christine Chichester, c.1910. Sulphur toned gelatine
silver print on rough textured paper.

bottom left 'Lashing' rye. This process removes the
grain, leaving the soft straw for thatching.
Christine Chichester, c.1910. Sulphur toned gelatine
silver print on rough textured paper.

above Michael Neill cleaning his cart.
Christine Chichester, c.1910. Gelatine silver printing
out paper.

THE LAND

Village of Duagh, Achill Island, County Mayo.
Around the time this photograph was taken Achill
was joined to the mainland, and thereafter
travellers, like the group of hunters shown in the
photograph, began to arrive in larger numbers.
But until then, there were few visitors to disrupt
the way of life.
Robert French, c.1890. Albumen print.

THE LAND

The fishery, Duagh, Achill. Buying and selling fish
on a stony beach in the north-west of Ireland.
Many of the men from Achill would have travelled
to Scotland or the north of England each year to
work on the harvest, leaving behind a largely
female society.
Robert French, c.1885. Albumen print.

TURF SLIDE-CAR WITH STRAW HARNESSED MOUNTAIN PONY, GLENDUN, CO.ANTRIM. R.W. 1544.

above Slide car with straw-harnessed mountain pony, Glendun, County Antrim. These wheel-less vehicles were used on farms throughout Ireland until the eighteenth century. After this they were found mainly in the northern counties. Ulster slide cars were characterised by the wooden runners fixed under the shafts, which could be replaced when necessary (similar vehicles in Scotland, Wales, Eastern Europe, Siberia, China and other places did not have this feature). Note the decoratively-woven straw harness.
Robert Welch, c.1895. Platinum print.

top right Farmyard scene, Glenshesk, County Antrim.
Robert Welch, c.1895. Platinum print.

right Street scene in Rostrevor, County Down. The similarities of construction between this wheel car and the slide cars in the previous images is clear.
Robert Welch, c.1895. Platinum print.

THE LAND

SLIDE-CAR FOR CORN, GLENSHESK, CO. ANTRIM. R.W. 1163.

AN OLD IRISH "LOW-BACK CAR" OR WHEEL-CAR, ROSTREVOR, CO. DOWN. R.W. 1756.

THE LAND

Funeral procession, County Kerry. There was an
old tradition that coffins should be carried to the
graveyard by the longest route possible, and should
encircle some place or object along the way, mov-
ing from east to west. Likewise, a grave should
never be dug on a Monday, unless it was unavoid-
able, people believed.
Christine Chichester, c.1910. Gelatine silver printing
out paper.

At the graveside in the same funeral as at left.
Roman travellers to Ireland are said to have found
a people who enjoyed their drink and were
addicted to funerals.
Christine Chichester, c.1910. Gelatine silver printing
out paper.

Threshers. Threshing machines, towed and
powered by steam tractors, were hired by the day
by reasonably prosperous farmers. Right up until
the 1960s the arrival of the threshing machine
remained a great annual event in farming
communities, with the children begging to be
allowed to stay home from school to watch the
excitement.
Unknown, c.1920. Modern contact print from
gelatine silver glass negative.

THE LAND

112

Lartigue Railway. From 1888 a monorail train (called after its designer, the French engineer Charles Lartigue) ran along a nine-mile stretch of track between the market town of Listowel and Ballybunion, on the coast, in County Kerry. The train was slow, never reaching more than about fifteen miles an hour, noisy and unsteady; the passengers, who sat on benches facing the windows, had to be distributed evenly, and balanced with iron weights. Financial difficulties dogged the project from the outset, and it is unlikely that the railway would have survived even had Ballybunion Station, several coaches and an engine not been blown up during the Civil War.

Christine Chichester, c.1910. Gelatine silver printing out paper.

THE LAND

Chapter Four

AT THE BIG HOUSE

The Irish 'Big House' was much more than a home for the family who owned it. It was a symbol, open to as many shades of interpretation as there were classes of Irishmen. To most of the Protestant Ascendancy the big house was the basis of their way of life and of civilisation in Ireland. To many of the native Irish it was a symbol of alien oppression. To others it provided employment, security and an identity. The country houses of Ireland ranged from the virtual palaces of the rich aristocracy, to the ramshackle manors of the hard-up squirearchy. But in the mid nineteenth century the Big House was almost invariably the centre of a world, with a network of dependents and with its own hierarchy, often apparently sustained with even more relish by the higher-up servants and employees than by the grandees themselves. The agent and the butler employed on a large estate were substantial people, often fiercely defending their territory, and their interests. Even in a more modest house, as far as the cook and the housekeeper were concerned the gulf between them and the outdoor servants was almost as significant as that between their employers and themselves.

They had a great power, these houses. Each had its own mythology, powerful amalgam of the family history, the architectural style of the house, and the *genius loci* , the spirit of the place. Distant relations might remain entranced by the magic of a house that they had visited only occasionally, and many families clung to homes they could barely afford to heat or maintain rather than sell them and move into comfortable and bland accommodation. Employees, and even local people who did not work on the estate, were often bound up in the mythology of a family and its house. Tales frequently abounded of, for example, the goodness of dowagers departed or of the sexual licentiousness of the landlord. Both were probably inaccurate, but in each the protagonist was drawn on a heroic scale and so his or her story usually acquired a special significance.

The tragedy of Ireland was that social divisions were artificially institutionalised by the religious divide. So the Protestant 'Anglo-Irish' were crystallized as a ruling caste entirely separate from the mass of the population, and yet they were increasingly robbed, by the masses they were meant to govern, of their identity as Irishmen. Most of the 'native' Irish, who had clung to the Catholic faith, had been prevented from participating fully in public life. The identity of each group was thus warped, to the detriment of both. In fact, the 'Anglo-Irish' included Norman families whose ancestors had arrived in Ireland in the twelfth century, as well as the descendants of successive waves of later settlers. Some 'Anglo-Irishmen' were the progeny of the relatively small number of Irish who had renounced the Catholic Church in order to advance themselves socially, and had assimilated into the Protestant world. Sir Jonah Barrington distinguished three types among the Anglo-Irish gentry in 1827: 'half-mounted gentry' (on familiar terms with servants but nevertheless admitted to Society, they usually carried lead-weighted whips in case they needed to scourge the peasantry), 'gentlemen every inch of them', and 'gentlemen to the backbone'.

left The Hon. Katie Dillon.
From a Crofton family album, 1860s. Albumen print.

'The Photo House' at Clonbrock.
This structure, which still stands, was an early darkroom and studio
used by member of the Dillon and Crofton families. It was built
specially for Augusta Crofton by her husband, who is shown in the photograph.
Augusta Crofton, c.1867. Albumen print.

Anglo-Irish attitudes to Ireland varied considerably. There were those who identified themselves with the country and its interests, and whose contribution to its achievements cannot be overlooked. The roll-call of distinguished Irishmen of the eighteenth and nineteenth centuries is largely composed of members of this class. Edmund Burke, George Berkeley, Oliver Goldsmith, Richard Brinsley Sheridan, Maria Edgeworth, Henry Grattan, Theobald Wolfe Tone, Jonathan Swift, Oscar Wilde and George Bernard Shaw were all products of Ascendancy backgrounds. Irish nationalism, until the twentieth century, was a largely Anglo-Irish cause. But there were also those who seemed to see the native Irish as a source of local colour and funny stories, providing much amusement when retold to family and friends, usually in a fake 'Oirish' accent which of itself provoked the giggles of boorish Anglo-Irish men and, far more vicious in their snobbery and racism, Anglo-Irish women.

Despite the apparent grandeur of many Irish country houses, money was frequently in rather short supply. In 1848, during the years of the famine, a quarter of Irish landlords were either insolvent or on the edge of bankruptcy. Much of the cost of the ineffective relief offered to the starving was dumped by the Westminster government on the Irish themselves. Some landowners further impoverished themselves attempting to help their hungry countrymen; others were content to ascribe starvation to native imprudence. By the time of the famine the old life of Ireland's ruling class was in any case under threat: the Ascendancy had been politically castrated by the Act of Union (1801). Then the Land Acts of the later nineteenth century dealt a mortal blow to many of the estates, severing large tracts of land. Acres that had been farmed by tenants were distributed to those who worked them. Admittedly, owners were generally decently compensated by the government, and some families were saved from financial ruin by the influx of money which enabled them to pay off old debts. But at the time the estates were purchased land prices were relatively lower than they had been before the famine, or than they were to be later. Much of the income from the purchase of land was badly invested, or simply spent. The real loss, however, was psychological, rather than financial. Without the bulk of their land, and effectively stranded on their modest personal holdings, the Anglo-Irish, and their way of life, became increasingly meaningless.

Labour was cheap, however, and it was possible to maintain a way of life that now seems impossibly grand with relatively little cash; in any event, an ability to overlook harsh reality when necessary to preserve peace of mind was one of the characteristics that united Irishmen of all classes. Although the Anglo-Irish might be able to persuade themselves that their position in Ireland was secure, most of them knew that they were seen by their friends and relations in England as slightly shabby eccentrics. All but the grandest appeared rather provincial at their schools, universities and regiments in England. This double sense of alienation, both in their native Ireland and in the England they never ceased to consider their mother country, undoubtedly contributed to the very strong sense of their identity as a separate caste. But although the Anglo-Irish knew that they were seen as interlopers in Ireland, few realised until the War of Independence the depth of hatred that the Irish lower middle class secretly cherished for them. Even then, as centuries of resentment erupted and about two hundred country houses were burned down, a great many employees and servants saved members of the owner's family, tried to rescue their property from the flames or guarded houses to prevent them being set alight. Landlords were surprised by the intensity of loyalty displayed in some incidents as much as by betrayal in others. Some of the families of the Ascendancy remained in Ireland, or returned after the Civil War. But their way of life had finally been destroyed. Hundreds of the houses they had lived in, whose architecture had been the towering achievement of post-Celtic Ireland in the visual arts, were razed to the ground, looted or, more often, simply left to decay.

AT THE BIG HOUSE

left Tower at Lismore Castle, County Waterford. This image is one of a series taken of renovations to Lismore which were planned by Sir Joseph Paxton, who designed the Crystal Palace for the Great Exhibition of 1851 in London. This series is one of the first in existence showing the stages of such work.
Francis Edmund Currey, 1854. Albumen print.

above Study of hanging game. For the Anglo-Irish upper classes in the nineteenth century country life revolved, to an even greater extent than in England, around the sports of shooting and hunting.
Francis Edmund Currey, c.1855. Albumen print.

AT THE BIG HOUSE

above Lord Clonbrock in theatrical costume.
Augusta Crofton, c.1865. Gold-toned albumen print.

top right Ladies of the Crofton and Tighe families
enjoying a country excursion.
Augusta Crofton, 1865. Albumen print.

bottom right Charlie Crofton.
Augusta Crofton, c.1858. Albumen print.

AT THE BIG HOUSE

AT THE BIG HOUSE

Group portrait. The careful composition reflects
Fitzgerald's conscious artistic intention to go
beyond the simple making of a record.
Lord Otho Fitzgerald, c.1855. Albumen print.

Lord Henry Gordon Lennox.
Augusta Crofton, 1858. Gold-toned albumen print.

above Clonbrock, County Galway. Lady Augusta
Crofton's home after her marriage. One of the
riders is identified as Mr Burton Persse,
Master of the local hunt.
Attributed to Augusta Crofton, c.1867. Albumen print.

opposite Children of the Tighe family.
L. Werner, Dublin, all c.1869. Hand-coloured and
gold-toned albumen prints.

AT THE BIG HOUSE

125

The Lion Gate at Mote Park, the Crofton family
home.
Attributed to Augusta Crofton, c.1859. Albumen print.

Castle Bernard, County Cork, the seat of the Earls
of Bandon. The Castle was burned down in 1921
during the War of Independence.
From an album compiled by Lady Bandon, c.1860.
Gold-toned albumen print.

Kilcornan, County Galway. Between the Act
of Union and the Famine there was a boom in
country-house building, in a great variety of styles.
Attributed to Augusta Crofton, c.1865. Albumen print.

AT THE BIG HOUSE

Kilronan Castle.
Attributed to Edward King-Tenison, c.1859.
Albumen print.

AT THE BIG HOUSE

top left Saloon, Powerscourt House, County
Wicklow. This was one of the grandest country-
house interiors in Ireland.
Robert French, 1890. Albumen print .

bottom left Rockingham, built for General Robert
King, the first Viscount Lorton, by Robert Nash
(subsequently architect to the Prince Regent) on the
shores of Lough Key in County Roscommon. The
house was conceived as a series of alternating
facades, without any visible back entrance.
An elaborate series of tunnels linked the house to

the stable-block, ice-house, canal and so on.
The demesne was laid out by Humphrey Repton,
one of the most famous garden architects of the
time, and like the house itself it was an attempt to
create an idealised world.
Unknown, 1858. Albumen print.

above Bantry House. Croquet, sedate and highly
suitable for the ladies, was a favourite game of the
gentry and aristocracy.
Unknown, from an album compiled by Lady Bandon,
1860s. Albumen print.

AT THE BIG HOUSE

above Augusta Crofton riding sidesaddle on her
horse Champion, ready for the hunt.
Unknown, 1860. Albumen print.

right Portrait of a lady and gentleman.
Lafayette, Dublin, 1890. Collodion silver printing
out paper.

AT THE BIG HOUSE

Bandon Cricket Club, Cork. Although gathered
to play the most English of games, there is
something quintessentially Irish about this group,
with its lackadaisical air.
Unknown, c.1860. Albumen print.

AT THE BIG HOUSE

A group of riders, possibly officers from a local regiment, before a point-to-point at Limerick in 1896. *Unknown*, 1896. Collodion silver printing out paper.

Chapter Five

IN THE TOWNS

The Industrial Revolution, which transformed cities, first in Britain then in other countries, in the nineteenth century, largely passed Ireland by. Poor communications, a shortage of investment capital, lack of fuel and the haemorrhage of talent that resulted from emigration prevented large-scale industrialisation. Ireland might be poor, but her towns were not, on the whole, blighted by the 'dark, Satanic mills' that reared over many of England's commercial centres. Nevertheless, the percentages of the population who were registered as living in towns increased from 18 per cent in 1851 to 33 per cent in 1911.

For good and for ill, however, Ulster did not escape the Industrial Revolution. In this, as in so many other instances, the northern counties proved to be the exception to the rule. In Belfast, Londonderry and other northern towns, the textile industry mechanised and boomed, despite the advent of cheap imported cotton in the early part of the century. By the early years of the twentieth century Belfast – 'Linenopolis' as it was sometimes called – had become the world's leading linen manufacturing and exporting base, providing employment for hundreds of thousands of workers in the mills and factories, including a very large number of women. Shipyards, tobacco factories and engineering and rope works also flourished in the city. Although the conditions were often uncomfortable, in steamy mills or crowded, noisy factories, these jobs gave women a degree of independence, and certainly affected the pattern of family life in communities where male unemployment was high. There were also seen to be great distinctions between the various occupations. So the women who worked in the weaving factories took a pride in what they saw as skilled work, undertaken in a fairly clean environment, compared to the rougher, dirtier work of the 'shawlies' in the spinning mills.

In Ireland, as elsewhere, small children were also regularly employed in factories. From the middle of the century, an eight-year-old was allowed to work ten hours a day, three days a week (attending the factory school on another two and a half days) and a twelve-year-old could be employed full time. Not only were the conditions in the factories unhealthy, but exhausted children were far more likely than adults to lose their concentration and injure themselves among the vast banks of noisy and dirty machinery, and a disabled child from a poor urban family faced almost certain destitution. Factory workers usually had two days' holiday at Christmas, two at Easter and two in July.

For Dublin, the first city of Ireland, the nineteenth century was a period of decline. As political Union with Great Britain robbed the city of its function as a capital, its prosperity declined and the living standards of a large percentage of its population slumped. Elegant streets and squares, built in the grand and yet accessible eighteenth-century Irish Georgian style, were rotting by 1900, turned into filthy tenements, teeming with families struggling for survival. Out of 5,000 such tenements, two-thirds were considered officially unfit for human habitation. Diseases such as tuberculosis, typhus and enteritis were endemic among the malnourished inhabitants of the overcrowded, damp tenements where thirty or more people shared a single water tap and foul lavatory. Dublin's slums had the highest mortality rate in

left Children of the tenements. Detail.
Christine Chichester, c.1910. See page 145.

Ryan's tobacco shop, Henry Street, Dublin.
Unknown. c.1900.
Gelatine silver printing out paper.

Europe. The gentry and the professional classes, not surprisingly, began to move out of the city. New suburbs such as Dalkey and Rathmines sprang up to the south of the city, where once there had been villages, and much of Dublin's prosperity followed their new inhabitants. Country people, unable to wrest a living from the land, flocked into the city, most of them ending up crammed meanly into the once gracious streets north of the River Liffey. Most would find the struggle for survival just as difficult as it had been back home, and living conditions in Dublin were infinitely more squalid than those in the countryside. Perhaps the one advantage, for a desperate man, was that it was easier to harbour an irrational optimism in the city; the opportunities for encountering a stroke of unexpected good luck were probably greater there. If they were lucky the new arrivals would survive as casual labourers, probably working at the docks, or as unskilled workers. This was not in general a good period for Dublin's industry. By the end of the century only breweries, distilleries and biscuit-factories were left as significant industrial employers. Jobs in these enterprises were keenly sought after, and vacancies tended to be filled by relations of those already on the payroll.

Social legislation aiming to improve the conditions of Ireland's rural poor was not paralleled by any concerted effort to help the most wretched Dubliners. Enquiries into the conditions of the slums were held, but these tended to achieve little more than record the appalling state of affairs. The Guinness brewing family were notable for their philanthropic initiatives, including the demolition of slums next to St Patrick's Cathedral to make way for flats, a library, a creche, a swimming pool, and a park. The City Authorities, however, were notable for their negligence, and even their corruption, over the question of housing the poor. In 1914 the *Enquiry into the Housing Conditions of Dublin's Working Classes* discovered that fourteen members of Dublin Corporation were owners or part owners of tenements. Further, two Aldermen, O'Reilly and Corrigan, had claimed tax rebates on the basis of improvements they had made to their properties, although they never actually carried out the work concerned.

In contrast to the callousness of the Corporation, the Viceroy, Lord Aberdeen, and particularly his wife, stand out as examples of decent concern for the well-being of Dubliners. Lord Aberdeen held the office of Viceroy in 1886 and again from 1906 until 1915. Irish Society found the Aberdeens dull; they entertained little, and without flair. But their commitment to helping the ordinary people of Ireland was made clear. In 1886 they asked garden party guests to wear clothes manufactured in Ireland, and after leaving the country they remained active in its affairs. Lady Aberdeen worked with the Congested Districts Board to encourage Irish industries and promote their products abroad. When the couple returned to Vice-Regal Lodge in 1906 Lady Aberdeen plunged herself into attempts to improve life for the urban poor. She established the Women's National Health Organisation, which set up clinics for babies, sanatoriums and playgrounds and she launched a health education campaign, aimed particularly at eradicating the scourge of tuberculosis, which killed 11,500 people a year in turn of the century Ireland. Her work in this field led the Nationalist Arthur Griffith to describe Lady Aberdeen as 'the Vice-Regal Microbe'.

Lectures, pamphlets and travelling exhibitions raised public awareness of the disease, which struck particularly at the vulnerable urban slum dwellers, although the middle and upper classes were also frequently affected. Among other measures to prevent the spread of tuberculosis and typhus, sterilised milk in sealed, one-meal containers was sold cheaply at special depots to the mothers of young children. Health visitors were employed to give basic instruction in hygiene and nutrition to city women, and although they were unable to resolve the difficulties faced by poor families in Dublin and Belfast, the health visitors undoubtedly alleviated the health risks and provided a valuable, reliable source of information on social conditions for the authorities and for religious and secular charities.

Charitable organisations attempted to tackle a wide range of social ills, and to encourage godliness among the benighted urban poor. Sunday schools and expeditions to the seaside were organised to provide wholesome recreation for urban women and children, and used clothing and boots were distributed to the most needy.

Unfortunately, well-meaning attempts to assist tenement families could be counter-productive. Philanthropists might stress the benefits of education, but conditions in city schools in the late nineteenth century were often fairly squalid, overcrowded and with inadequate lavatories. Many had neither playgrounds nor any facilities for physical training. It was not until the twentieth century that schools began to provide meals to supplement the inadequate diet many children received at home. Even if a slum child attended school until he was twelve, and even if he passed the employer's medical test, without family connections he was unlikely to get himself an apprenticeship – the key to the reasonably secure life of the skilled working class. Merely to survive into adulthood was something of a triumph for a poor urban youngster. Mortality was high among the tenement children, with 90 out of every 1,000 dying in the first year of life alone. The cost of burying a child, more than a week's wages for a labourer, added real hardship to a family's misery. But the shame of a pauper's burial for one of their children was so great that many families, scraping to survive at all, paid burial insurance to cover the cost of funerals. Despite the hardships facing Dublin's poor, the National Society for the Prevention of Cruelty to Children reported that they rarely had to touch parents in that city for ill-treating their offspring. This was in contrast to the situation they found in many English towns.

For the prosperous urban classes, in Dublin and Belfast as in the smaller towns of Ireland, the nineteenth century was a period of growing stability. Emancipation enabled the Catholic middle class to play a greater role in public and commercial life, and convent and monastic schools educated a new generation of Catholics to enter government service and the professions. Although Irish industry was not notably successful, commerce thrived in the nineteenth century, as trade with the rest of the British Isles and with the Empire brought a greater range of goods than ever before to the shops that were springing up all over Ireland. Family-run grocers, drapers and ironmongers, with confident name-boards adorning their expensive shop-fronts, bore witness to the entrepreneurial energy of the growing commercial caste.

O'Connell Street, Dublin. Amid the activity of a
large city, Dublin always retained its languid
elegance, and its humanity. The Irish writer and
politician Conor Cruise O'Brien is said to have
described it as 'a city where you can see a sparrow
falling to the ground, and God watching it'.
Robert French, c.1890. Albumen print.

O'Connell Bridge and Quays, Dublin. Horse-drawn trams were a familiar sight in Dublin for thirty years, until the beginning of the twentieth century. The Dublin United Tramways Company ordered the crews to keep a lookout for potential passengers, and catch their attention, in the hope of inducing them to take the tram rather than walk. *Unknown*, c.1885. Gold-toned albumen print.

Penny dinners. State provision for the poor was very limited, and most of the available relief came from the many charitable organisations, most of them run by the Churches. Despite the work of these organisations, most of Dublin's poor lived on a diet of bread and tea, and thought themselves lucky if they were not actually hungry on any given day.

Christine Chichester, c.1910. Gelatine silver printing out paper.

Children of the tenements. At the turn of the century nearly a quarter of the population of Dublin lived in one room, with an average of six people per room. A building with one hundred inhabitants usually had two lavatories, and only one third of Dublin tenements were considered fit for human habitation.

Christine Chichester, c.1910. Gelatine silver printing out paper.

12th July. The annual Orange March in Belfast, commemorating the Protestant King William of Orange's victory over the Catholic James II in the Battle of the Boyne (1690). Around the time of the photograph, the threat of Home Rule was bringing middle-class businessmen and professionals into the traditionally working, or lower middle class Orange Lodges.

Robert Welch, 1888. Toned albumen print.

PROCESSION PASSING THROUGH SHAFTESBURY   R.W.

Albert Memorial, Belfast. The pace of life in
bustling, industrial Belfast was very different from
that in the more leisurely Dublin. This was not
surprising, since Dublin was an ancient town that
had grown over the centuries, whereas Belfast
had expanded very rapidly on the back of
industrialisation. It acquired the status of
a city in 1888.
Robert French, c.1890. Albumen print.

IN THE TOWNS

Loading up a coach in the streets of Greyabbey, on
the Ards peninsula, County Down. The coach
passengers are probably on an excursion from
Belfast.
J. Phillips, Belfast, c.1895. Varnished gelatine silver
printing out paper.

IN THE TOWNS

left Market, Eyre Square, Galway.
From Charles Johnston 'Ireland Through the Stereoscope,'
published by Underwood & Underwood as one of
a stereo pair collection, c.1900. Gelatine silver
printing out paper.

above Workmen of Harland & Wolff's shipyard
leave to make their way home.
Attributed to Robert Welch, c.1912. Toned gelatine
silver print.

IN THE TOWNS

IN THE TOWNS

top left Propeller, Harland & Wolff, Belfast. The shipyard, bought by Edward Harland in 1858, and subsequently developed with his partner, Gustav Wolff, was to become the largest in the world for a time. It covered a 120-acre (50 hectare) site on the Lagan, and was a major employer for the Protestant (but usually not the Catholic) working class of the city. Among the ships built here was the ill-fated *Titanic*. For an indication of the scale of this propeller, note the figure standing on the left. *Attributed to Robert Welch*, c.1910. Gelatine silver developing out paper.

bottom left A young apprentice looks out from inside a boiler section in the workshops at Harland & Wolff. *Attributed to Robert Welch*, c.1864. Developed out gelatine silver transparency.

above The launch of the liner *Olympic* from Harland's yard in Belfast. The *Olympic* was a sister to the *Titanic*. *Unknown*, 20 October 1910. Developed out gelatine silver transparency.

IN THE TOWNS

left Waterford Harbour. Note the sailors working
on the yardarm of the vessel to the left of the clock
tower.
Ringrose Atkins, September 1894. One of a stereo
pair, toned gelatine silver transparency.

above The Quays, Drogheda, with waterside idlers
content to watch the photographer at work.
Robert French, c.1885. Albumen print.

IN THE TOWNS

155

A steam tram (a chimney is visible between the two
sections of the carriage) of the Cavehill and
Whitewell Tramway, Belfast.
Robert Welch, c.1890. Albumen print.

St Patrick's Bridge and a paddle steamer at the
quay, Cork. Cork City was originally built on an
island but it soon expanded on to the banks of the
River Lee.
Robert French, c. 1890. Albumen print.

IN THE TOWNS

top left Passengers prepare for their journey on
Bianconi's Galway-Clifden Mail Car. Charles
Bianconi, an Italian by birth, created a large
coaching and transport concern in Ireland,
beginning in 1815. Later he was also prominent in
the development of Irish railways.
Robert French, 1880s. Albumen print.

left Passenger carts in the main street of Kenmare.
Robert French, 1890s. Albumen print with blue
aniline dye.

above A young delivery boy stands nonchalantly in
the main street of Claremorris, County Mayo.
Thomas Wynne, 1871. Albumen print.

IN THE TOWNS

above A group of Passionist priests at the
Maynooth seminary.
Unknown, c.1895. Platinum print.

right An open air Mass at the shrine of Our Lady
at Knock, where the faithful report many
miraculous cures. Note the crutches fixed to the
wall of the Church, abandoned by disabled people
who believed themselves cured and, it is said,
returned home unaided.
Unknown, c.1885. Albumen print.

IN THE TOWNS

Chapter Six

REVIVAL & REVOLUTION

Ireland was rediscovering herself during the second half of the nineteenth century. Politicians, artists and intellectuals were all engaged, in their various ways, in addressing the question of what it meant to be Irish.

There were at this time two strains within Irish nationalism. First there was the element that stressed the tradition of 1798 and of Wolfe Tone, a strain that found its voice in the Young Ireland movement, demanding an independent Republic, and probably radical agrarian reform. The second strain was represented by the Irish Party at Westminster, where for the first time a group of MPs defined themselves by their interest in the affairs of Ireland. Throughout the century these two intertwined strains struggled to decide Ireland's future. J.G. Biggar, elected to Westminster in 1874, was even thrown out of the Irish Republican Brotherhood for his Parliamentary activities. This was in spite of the fact that his insistence on strict party discipline, turning the Irish faction into a force to reckoned with, inspired the other parties in the House of Commons and provided the example upon which the rigid discipline of modern party whips is based. Biggar, an Ulster businessman who converted to Catholicism, advocated obstruction rather than cooperation as the Irish Party's key to achieving its ends at Westminster. Nevertheless, the IRB could not forgive his collusion with the Parliamentary establishment.

The 'New Departure', brokered late in 1878 by the Fenian John Devoy and Charles Stewart Parnell, brought the two strains in Irish nationalism together, and enabled the revolutionaries and the constitutionalists to cooperate in their efforts to achieve Irish independence, despite deep mutual mistrust. This agreement more or less coincided with another failure in the potato crop and a depression in British agricultural prices as more American produce was imported. Without their staple food, and without any possibility of casual farm work in England or Scotland, people in the west of Ireland were once again faced with starvation. The scale of the tragedy could not be compared with that of the great hunger thirty years earlier, but the hardship was real, and rents certainly could not be paid. Families were evicted from their homes, and violent reprisals against the landlords followed. Cases of cattle-burning appeared to outrage public opinion in England more than the callous eviction of a hungry family from their smallholding. (The landlord's cattle were resented as a 'cash crop' that did

left Charles Kickham (1828-82), novelist and poet.
The son of a prosperous County Tipperary shopkeeper,
Kickham was almost blind and totally deaf after a shooting accident in his youth.
He joined Young Ireland and, in about 1860, the Fenians,
the Republican movement named after the legendary Fionn Mac Cumhail's band of warriors.
Kickham proved effective in internal Fenian disputes, was appointed
to the supreme executive of the organisation,
and became joint editor of its newspaper, the *Irish People*.
In 1865 he and other Fenians were betrayed by an informer.
Kickham was sentenced to fourteen years penal servitude
but after four years he was released in poor health.
Lauder Brothers, Dublin, c.1863. Albumen print.

An Irish army armoured car in action
in Dublin at the outbreak of the Civil War.
Unknown, 1922. Modern contact print
from a glass negative.

nothing to feed the poor.) The land problem once again appeared central to Irish politics, but where once the aim had been to give the tenant security, now the belief was taking root that only when the farmer owned his land would he be safe.

The Land Act of 1881 theoretically gave tenants greater security, but it was impossibly complicated, and failed to tackle all the issues involved. Agrarian violence continued. Charles Stewart Parnell, leader of the Irish Party in Parliament, was aware that the Act represented an improvement on previous legislation, and facilitated its passage. Mindful of the demands of his more radical followers, however, he publicly denounced the Act, and was accused by Prime Minister Gladstone of 'marching through rapine to the dismemberment of the Empire', although unlike many members of his party he had not been personally involved in the violent outrages. He was imprisoned without trial for seven months in Kilmainham Jail until, under the terms of the so-called 'Kilmainham Treaty', he and Land League leaders were released from prison, tenants' outstanding rents were amnestied, and the Land Act would be amended in return for Parnell exerting his influence to bring an end to the violence.

After the Land Act and the 'Treaty' the main objective for Nationalists became Home Rule. In the 1885 General Election the Home Rulers won every Irish seat except those representing East Ulster and Trinity College, Dublin (which was then an exclusively Protestant institution). They then allied themselves with the Conservatives and brought down the government. Parnell was prepared to forge alliances with whichever Westminster Party seemed most likely to help his cause, but after the second 1885 election Lord Salisbury forfeited any hope of retaining Irish Party support to keep him in office, by announcing the introduction of a Coercion Bill, granting the Government emergency powers to deal with unrest.

Another government fell, and Mr Gladstone returned to power, only to resign the following year after the defeat of the Home Rule Bill. In their campaign to defeat Home Rule Joseph Chamberlain and Lord Randolph Churchill (Winston Churchill's father) first advanced the argument that there were really two Irelands, and that the Protestants of the North could not be expected to live under native Irish rule: 'Ulster will fight and Ulster will be right'. The slogan first used by Churchill to stir up the Belfast Orangemen in 1886 was to become the watchword of the Unionists of Ulster. Within weeks of Churchill's speech 73,000 Orangemen had volunteered to fight Home Rule, by force if necessary. Arms were bought, and drilling followed. There was no need to implement the threat of violence, this time, but the scene was set for future bloodshed.

Parnell's disgrace, following the revelation of his affair with Mrs O'Shea, splitting the Irish Party and ending Gladstone's cooperation with the Home Rulers, was an appalling blow for Irish political aspirations. For the artists and intellectuals who were becoming involved in the quest for an Irish identity, the tragedy of Parnell, the noble spirit brought low by the envy of lesser men, almost seemed to encapsulate his country's despair. Briefly, a degree of independence had seemed almost to be within grasp, but this hope had been doomed along with so many others.

Politics and art were becoming increasingly intertwined. The revival of interest in the Gaelic culture and language had a profound influence on Irish literature after Parnell, and inspired the new generation of Nationalist activists. The Gaelic League, founded in 1893 by the Protestant Douglas Hyde, later to be Ireland's first President, and the Catholic Eoin MacNeill, who was to establish the Irish Volunteers twenty years later, counted almost all the entire Irish Republican Brotherhood among its members. Like the Gaelic Athletic Association, whose volunteers drilled using hurley sticks in place of rifles, the Gaelic League provided a cover for Nationalist activities. Indeed, after the failure of the 1916 Rising, the League offered a vital front behind which Nationalists could group. The real legacy of the League, however, was the imagery it bequeathed to Irish patriots, providing a new mythology for the Nationalist movement after the indignity of the fall of Parnell. The rediscovery of the Gaelic heritage also offered a reinvigorated cultural identity to the Catholic population, although this was only a step away from a patronisingly quaint interpretation of peasant life. With characteristic Irish ambivalence, both Yeats and Joyce, the two great geniuses associated with the Irish literary revival, recognised the petty provincialism of the movement, even as they were swept along by its romance. But there is no doubt that the movement encouraged the development of nationalist feeling, and many of its lesser literary talents were political activists. These included the mystic Joseph Mary Plunkett, and also Padraig Pearse, whose romantically despairing poetry encapsulates a spirit that pervaded much of Europe, as well as Ireland, on the eve of the First World War. Pearse's painful awareness of the supposed need for blood sacrifice to purge society echoes the anguished heroism of the English First World War poets.

The question of Home Rule for Ireland fell from sight for some years after Parnell's disgrace. It was not until 1910, when support from Irish MPs was needed to push Lloyd George's budget through Parliament, that the issue came to the forefront once more. The price for Irish help was the Parliament Act of 1911, restricting the powers of the House of Lords. This decreed that the Upper Chamber could only delay the passage of a bill twice; thereafter it could become law without their support. The Third Irish Home Rule Bill was passed by the Commons in 1912, and duly rejected by the Lords, and the process was repeated in 1913. In 1914, therefore, it was to come into force despite their lordships' opposition. But the Unionists remained adamant in their opposition to Home Rule and they were armed. In April the Ulster Volunteers succeeded in bringing 30,000 rifles into Ireland without interference from the authorities, in what came to be known as the Larne Gun-Running incident.

By this time both Nationalists and Unionists were drilling openly, the former without the same cooperation from the authorities. The mood of Irish nationalism was now shifting decisively away from constitutional action and towards revolutionary fervour. Sinn Fein advocated setting up a parliament in Dublin, without waiting for the passage of the Home Rule Bill. The so-called Curragh Mutiny in March 1914, in which 58 British officers, stationed at the Curragh near Dublin, threatened to resign from the army rather than take part in coercing Ulster to succumb to Home Rule was a demonstration of Westminster's feebleness in the face of Unionist threats. The Secretary for War, Sir John Seely, assured the officers that the army would not be asked to crush political opposition. Prime Minister Asquith sacked Seely and repudiated his undertaking, but the officers remained in their posts. Asquith was, in any case, politically enfeebled by this time, struggling to hold a divided Cabinet together, and the monarch, King George V, had let his sympathy for the Unionist cause be known.

In May 1914 the House of Commons passed the Home Rule Bill for the third time. The four mainly Protestant counties of the north – Antrim, Armagh, (London-)Derry and Down – insisted that they would not agree to be ruled from Dublin. In July John Redmond, leader of the Irish Nationalist Party, apparently conceded that these counties should be excluded from Home Rule. The Unionists then insisted that two more counties, whose population was at least half Catholic, Fermanagh and Tyrone, should also be excluded. Redmond could not have carried his party had he agreed to this. The Howth incident on 26 July raised the tension in Ireland still further. Nationalist gun runners, including the popular novelist Erskine Childers and a distinguished Dublin surgeon, Sir Thomas Myles, managed to import 1,500 rifles, despite the efforts of the army to prevent them. A large crowd, angered that the official blind eye turned towards Unionists illegally importing arms was not extended to the Nationalists, began stoning the troops who opened fire, killing three people and injuring another 38. Ireland was on the brink of civil war, and Redmond and Asquith were under great pressure to agree a compromise. International affairs were demanding ever more attention. Europe was mobilising on an unprecedented scale. By the time Redmond and Asquith reached agreement, war with Germany had broken out. The Home Rule Bill was passed with two provisos: that it would not come into effect until the world war ended, and until Parliament had been able to consider special provision for Ulster.

At the height of its prosperity and global influence Europe had plunged into a conflict that was to become the worst in history to that time. Now, more than ever, the question of Ireland could be nothing but an irritant for Britain. But to some in Ireland, where whole families had starved to death within living memory, where Nationalist aspirations seemed once more doomed to disappointment just when they appeared to be satisfied, this was the final straw. Redmond, in agreeing to Westminster's terms, had abandoned the Nationalist cause to extra-Parliamentary forces.

By September 1914 there were 180,000 Irish Volunteers. Redmond had indicated that they would be used for the defence of Ireland, but that month he urged them to join the British forces. Nine out of ten appeared to respond to this appeal (and most of the Ulster Volunteers similarly enlisted). The rest of the Nationalists came under the control of the Irish Republican Brotherhood, led by Padraig Pearse, Thomas MacDonagh and Joseph Plunkett. The IRB, with its leadership of romantic Irish Catholic gentlemen, was invigorated in January 1916 by the admission of James Connolly, a Marxist agitator with much needed organisational skills. Connolly agreed to cooperate with a rising that was being planned for Easter 1916. The debate among Nationalists at the time was whether no rebellion should be planned unless it had a reasonable chance of success (the argument of Eoin MacNeill, commander of the Volunteers) or whether an enterprise which might fail, but that showed that Irishmen were willing to die for their freedom, would rouse their countrymen's conscience.

Although preparations for the Rising seemed to be cursed, on Easter Monday 1916 about 1,600 men took on the British Empire. The centre of their operations was the General Post Office in O'Connell Street in Dublin, where the formation of the Provisional Government of the Irish Republic was proclaimed. The Rising lasted five days. Some 1,350 people, including soldiers and civilians, were killed or seriously wounded. Fifteen of the leaders were shot, and Sir Roger Casement, the Foreign Office civil servant who had sought help from Germany and returned to Ireland by submarine, was caught and hanged for treason. Armed rebels during a time of war could expect no other treatment. The leaders of the Easter Rising were not benighted slum dwellers like the wretched followers of the adventurer Emmet. Theirs had been a calculated operation. Their deaths galvanised Irish support not just for Home Rule, but for complete independence. Public opinion among Irish Americans was also aroused on behalf of Sinn Fein, and of the Irish Republican Army which it launched.

Lloyd George made one last attempt to find a solution to the problem. He persuaded Edward Carson and the Unionists to agree to Home Rule for the 26 southern counties, so long as the North was to be exempt, and he gave Redmond to understand, on the contrary, that the exclusion of the North would be only temporary. Thus he thought that he could separate Home Rulers from Sinn Fein supporters, and placate the Unionists. The deal would never have held, but the knowledge of it finally destroyed Redmond's authority in Ireland.

In the December 1918 General Election Sinn Fein won 73 out of 105 Irish constituencies. Refusing to take their seats at Westminster the Sinn Fein MPs, considering themselves to have been elected as the Parliament of an independent country, established the first Dail in Dublin, with Eamon de Valera as their leader. At the same time the first shots were being fired in what was to become known as the War of Independence. On 21 January 1919 members of the Third Tipperary Brigade of the Irish Volunteers ambushed and killed two officers of the Royal Irish Constabulary, who were escorting explosives to a quarry in Tipperary. Throughout the year the level of the violence increased. In February 1920 the British government introduced a revised version of the Third Home Rule Bill, partitioning Ireland and establishing one Parliament in the South, and another, Stormont, in the North. Sinn Fein rejected the deal. They wanted complete independence, not just Home Rule, and they wanted it for all 32 counties. The fighting was bloody, with atrocity following atrocity on each side.

By the summer of 1921 Lloyd George was under pressure to find a solution, from the King, who urged conciliation, from the Labour Party and from the Liberals. The Irish, on all sides, were exhausted from the struggle. On 6 December 1921 a treaty was signed, by Arthur Griffith, Michael Collins and others on behalf of the Dail, accepting partition and Dominion status for Southern Ireland within the British Commonwealth.

The troubles were still not over. Neither Dominion status, nor membership of the Commonwealth, nor the partition of Ulster were acceptable to the most committed Republicans. De Valera and his followers left the Dail, and Arthur Griffith was elected President. Former comrades-in-arms had to decide where they stood on this latest painful refinement of the question of Ireland's political future. Michael Collins and the IRB were 'free-Staters', prepared to accept the Treaty. De Valera, Cathal Brugha and others opposed it at any cost. The anti-Treatyites seized the Four Courts on 13 April 1922 and Civil War began in earnest on 28 June when government troops moved against the occupants. Again war raged throughout Ireland until the summer of 1923 but in May of that year de Valera issued a statement conceding defeat.

Six or seven hundred people are believed to have lost their lives in the South during the Civil War. There were over 450 further deaths in the North in sectarian violence also, with thousands more being forced out of their homes or losing their jobs. The cost in damage to life and property on both sides of the new border was very high, and in the legacy of bitterness that has scarred Ireland since, incalculable.

Constance Markievicz (née Gore-Booth),
Nationalist. Countess Markievicz fought in the
1916 Rising and was elected as Sinn Fein MP for St
Patrick's Dublin in the 1918 election, the first
woman to be elected to the British parliament,
although like the other Sinn Fein MPs she did not
take her seat.
Lafayette Dublin, c.1890.
Gelatine silver transparency.

top left James Stephens (1824-1901), founder of the Irish Republican Brotherhood. A civil engineer on the Limerick and Waterford Railway, Stephens joined the Young Ireland movement and took part in the 1848 rising at Ballingarry, County Tipperary, in which he was wounded. Exaggerated reports of his death enabled him to evade the authorities and escape to France, where he lived until 1856. In that year he returned to Ireland and began travelling around setting up an underground network of reliable contacts. During this period he was known as *'an seabhac siubhalach'* ('the wandering hawk'), anglicised to 'Shooks'. The IRB, started on 17 March 1858, was organised on military lines, in 'circles' of 820 men, each answerable to its own colonel or 'centre'. On the same day, in New York, Stephens' friend John O'Mahony established the Fenians as an American auxiliary organisation, and members of the IRB itself rapidly became known as 'Fenians'. Stephens was a vigorous campaigner, but Republicans in Ireland and America were irritated by his high-handed approach, exaggerating active support for the movement in Ireland, and endlessly complaining that he was receiving inadequate help from the Americans. The movement was also divided over the question of an armed rising. In 1866 Stephens was described by the American Fenians as 'a rogue, impostor and traitor' and sacked as Head Centre. He lived in Paris and Switzerland until, with the help of Parnell he was enabled to return to Ireland in 1886, where he lived out his life quietly at Blackrocks, County Dublin. *Unknown*, 1866. Albumen print.

top right Mary Eva Kelly (1826-1910), poet and Nationalist.
Robert French, Dublin, 1860s. Albumen print.

bottom Kevin Izod O'Doherty (1823-1905), a Dubliner who joined 'Young Ireland' while at medical school. This was a mainly middle-class nationalist movement, aspiring to 'internal union and external independence'. In 1849 O'Doherty was sentenced to ten years transportation to Van Diemen's land (later Tasmania). He was engaged to be married to Mary Eva Kelly, who wrote poetry for the *Nation* and other newspapers under the pen-name 'Eva', but when convicted he told her that she should consider herself free of the commitment. However, she refused the offer, and remained loyal to his memory, until he returned to Dublin in 1854 with a pardon, and married her. He qualified as a doctor and later emigrated to Brisbane, where he became actively engaged in politics, serving as a member of the Queensland legislative assembly from 1877 to 1885.
J.H. Burke, Dublin, 1860s. Albumen print .

above William Murphy, a former Catholic, lectured against 'Popery' in England in the 1860s when, especially in the aftermath of Fenian activities, there were riots between Irish Catholics and Orangemen in a number of towns.
Unknown, 1866. Albumen print.

opposite top left Hugh McGriskin, Fenian prisoner. *Prison photograph,* 31 May 1865. Gold-toned albumen print.

opposite top right James Donaghy, Fenian prisoner. *Prison photograph,* 1866. Gold-toned albumen print.

bottom right John O'Leary (1830-1907), Republican. W.B. Yeats, bitter and disillusioned at the self-righteousness and materialism of Irish society, used O'Leary, in his great poem, 'September 1913' as the symbol of the lost purity of Irish nationalism:
'Romantic Ireland's dead and gone,
It's with O'leary in the grave.'
O'Leary had been imprisoned for Republican activities and was a mentor to many of the younger generation of Irish nationalist artists and intellectuals, including Katharine Tynan, Maud Gonne and Douglas Hyde, as well as Yeats.
Unknown, 1860s. Albumen print.

left Captain Charles Cunningham Boycott (1832-97) was the land agent of Lord Erne in County Mayo. He opposed the Land League in its demand for rent reductions, and was one of the earliest victims of the policy, first advocated by John Dillon in 1879, and a year later espoused by Parnell, of 'moral Coventry'. The local people refused to work for him. Boycott's crops were saved by a work force of fifty Orangemen, who were escorted by over one thousand troops during the two weeks it took to bring in the harvest. The Boycott Relief Expedition cost the government £10,000, or as Parnell said, 'one shilling for every turnip dug'. On 13 December 1880 the *Daily Mail* described the new tactic of the Land League as 'boycott', thus immortalising the Captain. The photo dates from Boycott's participation with various English political leaders in a shoot at Hampstead, near London, in the 1860s.
Bullock Brothers, Leamington, 1863. Albumen print.

above left Michael Davitt (1846-1906). Agrarian agitator, nationalist and journalist. Working in a Lancashire cotton-mill, Davitt's right arm was torn off by machinery when he was ten years old; the family had moved to England to look for work after they were evicted in 1850. He joined the IRB, and was chief arms procurer for the Fenians until 1870, when he was imprisoned. He served seven years, then travelled to the United States before returning home to Mayo, where he was instrumental in founding the Land League of Mayo. As far as Davitt was concerned, the slogan 'the land for the people' meant nationalisation, but to the tenants themselves, ownership of the land was the goal.
Unknown, 1880. Woodbury type.

above right Lord Frederick Cavendish, assassinated by nationalists in Phoenix Park in Dublin in 1882 on the day he had been sworn in as Chief Secretary. The real target was the Under-Secretary, Thomas Burke, who was also killed.
Unknown, c.1880. Woodbury type.

'Shadowing' in Tipperary. Father Humphries
(1834-1930), a priest who supported the Land
League, and organised a rent strike in Tipperary,
shown with the 'shadows' charged openly to watch
his every movement by the government.
Unknown, 1890s. Collotype.

Charles Stewart Parnell (1846-91), statesman, entered the British Parliament in 1875, becoming leader of the Home Rule Confederation in 1879 and President of the Land League. In the General Election of April 1880, sixty-one MPs committed to Home Rule were returned to Westminster, and Parnell was elected chairman of the Home Rule Party. In August he was suspended from Parliament for encouraging the Land League, and in October he was arrested. Prime Minister Gladstone came to terms with Parnell, in the 'Kilmainham Treaty' (called after the Dublin jail in which Parnell was imprisoned) in March 1882, in a deal brokered by Captain William O'Shea, a Home Rule MP, and his wife Kitty. According to this, land reform continued but agitation was to stop. The 1885 General Election was a triumph for Parnell, whose party, pledged to struggle for independence by legal means, won every Irish seat outside Dublin University and Eastern Ulster, and held the balance of power at Westminster. Parnell's victory convinced Gladstone of the case for Home Rule; he supported it for the rest of his career. In 1890 Captain O'Shea divorced Kitty, citing her adultery with Parnell. Many who otherwise supported Home Rule thought this divorce was disgraceful and Gladstone was forced to ask Parnell to stand down as leader of the Irish Party. Parnell refused, and split the Party. He died in Brighton, less than five months after he had married Mrs O'Shea.

Robert French, 1889. Albumen print with aniline dye.

left Turlogh McSweeney, 'the Donegal piper'.
One of the most famous nineteenth-century Irish
pipers, he was the son and grandson of pipers, and
was anxious to follow their example. However,
'there was no music in me', he explained later, until
he appealed to the fairies, who inspired him to
play. Despite this romantic musical education,
McSweeney was noted for his reserved and
dignified manner, uncommon in a musician. The
scholar John O'Donovan described watching the
family in 1835: '[the group]... consisted of a man,
tall and stately, three women and some children
accompanied by a hampered ass, some greyhounds
and other dogs... What group, said I, addressing
the fisherman, is this on the strand? That, said he,
is May Swyne na Doe and his family, the heir of
Doe Castle and the Sinsear of the Clann Suivne,
who though he retains all the high notions of his
forebears, has been obliged to exchange the sword
and battle-axe for the budget and the soldering iron
... and the spirited, richly caparisoned steed for the
tame and rudely hampered ass. The only badge of
his nobility are now his greyhounds and dogs, of
which no petty game hunters have dared to deprive
him, for Captain Hart treats him with great
respect, and delights to hear him romancing about
the daring achievements... of Sir Malmurry Mac
Swinnedo, from whom, in a direct line, he is the
fifth in descent.' Turlogh was one of the children
referred to in this account. Towards the end of the
nineteenth century there was considerable interest
in traditional Irish music; McSweeney was even
taken to Chicago to play for the people waiting to
enter the World's Fair in Chicago in 1893.
Attributed to 'Mac an tSaoir', 1911. Developed out
gelatine silver print.

above Irish piper. Hand in hand with the development of political nationalism in the later nineteenth
century was a growth of interest in all aspects of
Gaelic Irish culture in music, literature, sport and
other areas.
Unknown, c.1905. Gelatine silver printing out paper.

Members of the Ulster Volunteer Force, founded in 1913, to oppose Home Rule which was due to become law the following year. 'Drilling is illegal', Edward Carson, the leading Ulster politician, said, 'The Volunteers are illegal and the government knows they are illegal, and the government does not interfere with them.' Here, the force is armed with Martini Enfield .303 carbines. The figure on the right appears to be a Boer War veteran, judging by his decorations.
Unknown, c.1914. Gelatine silver print developing out paper.

Sean McDermott (1884-1916). McDermott was a
leading organiser of the IRB and was executed
after the 1916 Easter Rising in which he had been a
prominent figure.
Unknown, c.1914. Gelatine silver developed out
print.

REVIVAL & REVOLUTION

above O'Connell Street and Bridge following the
Easter Rising.
Unknown, 1916. Gelatine silver developed out print.

right Damage in Dublin following the Easter
Rising of 1916. James Connolly was the leader of
the Irish Transport & General Workers' Union
and its head office, shown in the photograph,
briefly became Liberty Hall during the Rising. The
same building was also the head office of the Irish
Women Workers' Union, founded by Delia
Larkin, sister of the leading Nationalist, James
Larkin.
Chancellor, Dublin, 1916. Gelatine silver developed
out print.

overleaf An incident in Dublin during the War of
Independence. The location of the photograph is
Easons bookshop at the corner of Abbey Street and
O'Connell Street. Spectators run for cover as
trouble begins for the convoy of British soldiers and
Black and Tans.
Unknown, 1921. Gelatine silver developed out print.

left British security forces. A policeman, soldier
and two Black and Tans.
W. Hogan, c.1921. Gelatine silver developed out
print.

above A group of British Intelligence operatives
known as the Cairo gang. All were killed in an
IRA operation planned by Michael Collins, being
simultaneously attacked at a variety of locations in
Dublin on 20 November 1920. The day later
became known as 'Bloody Sunday' after Black and
Tans fired on a football crowd in retaliation.
Unknown, 1920. Gelatine silver developed out print.

REVIVAL & REVOLUTION

top left Balbriggan, Dublin, after the Black and
Tans had sacked the district in revenge for the
shooting of a senior police officer. In the course of
this raid two local people were bayonetted to death.
The Black and Tans, 7,000 demobilised soldiers,
recruited from Britain to support the Royal Irish
Constabulary during the War of Independence,
began to arrive in Ireland in March 1920. They
were issued with khaki trousers and dark green
tunics, a uniform reminiscent of a famous fox hunt,
the Scarteen Black and Tans. Six thousand
Auxiliaries, recruited from ex-officers and somewhat better disciplined, followed later the same
year. The violence of both groups outraged liberal
British opinion as well as provoking greater support
for Republicans in Ireland and many reprisals from
Republicans also.
Unknown, 1920. Gelatine silver print.

bottom left Funeral of Terence MacSwiney
(1879-1920), the Mayor of Cork, who died at
Brixton Prison in London after a hunger-strike of
seventy-four days.
Unknown, 1920. Gelatine silver developing out
paper. Enlargement, probably from a copy
negative.

above One image from a sequence shot during a
famous incident during the War of Independence.
Sean Tracy of the IRA's Tipperary Brigade shot
and killed two British officers in Talbot Street,
Dublin, before himself being killed. Here, one of
the casualties is being carried away.
Unknown, 1920. Gelatine silver print, developing out
paper. Enlargement from a copy negative.

The changing of the guard. Departing British
troops hand over to the new Irish army at a Dublin
barracks.
Unknown, 1922. Modern print from a glass
negative.

British troops march to the ships that will take
them from Ireland, the North Wall, Dublin.
Unknown, 1922. Modern print from a glass
negative.

During the Civil War several attempts were made to secure a truce. Seen here, at the Mansion House in Dublin, the men who negotiated one ceasefire, which was to hold for a little more than a fortnight. Left to right: General MacEoin (1893-1973, Free State); Sean Moylan (1888-1957, IRA); General O'Duffy (1892-1944, Free State); Liam Lynch (1890-1923, IRA, shot by government troops in the Knockmealdown Mountains); Gearoid O'Sullivan (Free State) and Liam Mellows (1892-1922, IRA, executed by the provisional Government). *Unknown*, 1922. Modern print from a glass negative.

A train derailed by IRA action at Cloghjordan,
County Tipperary, during the Civil War.
Unknown, 1922-3. Gelatine silver developed out
print.

REVIVAL & REVOLUTION

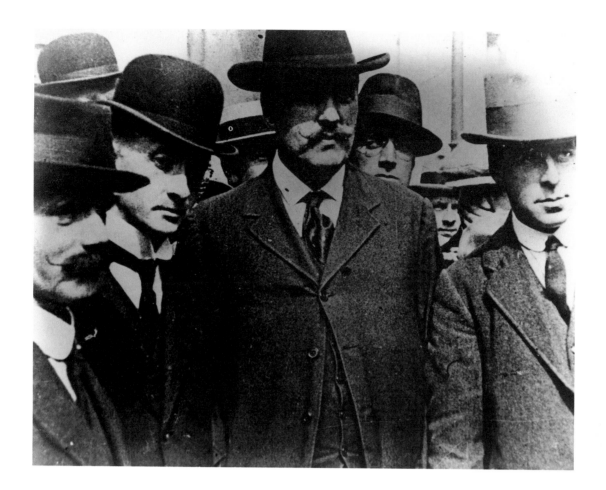

top left First Aid Unit, 4th Battalion, Mid-Clare Brigade of the IRA.
Unknown, 1921. Gelatine silver printing out paper.

bottom left Eamon de Valera (1882-1975). Statesman. New York-born de Valera was sentenced to death in 1917 for his part in the Easter Rising of 1916, but the sentence was commuted and 'Dev' became an MP and President of Sinn Fein. He was arrested again, and escaped from Lincoln Jail with the help of Michael Collins and Harry Boland in 1919. He authorised the negotiations of 1921 with the British, but could not countenance the Treaty because it provided for partition of Ireland. When, on 7 January 1922, the Dail voted by 64 to 57 for the Treaty, de Valera wept at what he saw as the betrayal of the Republican ideal. During the Civil War de Valera was arrested by the Free State government. In 1926 he formed a new Party, *Fianna Fail* ('Soldiers of Destiny'), and later served as Prime Minister and then President of the Irish Republic.
Hartsook, San Francisco, c.1922. Gelatine silver developing out paper. Enlargement.

above Civil War leaders: William Cosgrove (centre left) and Sean O'Mahony (centre right).
Unknown, 1922. Gelatine silver developing out paper.

General Michael Collins. Photo by Hogan Dubli

Michael Collins (1890-1922). Soldier and politician. During the Easter Rising of 1916 Collins served as aide-de-camp to Joseph Plunkett in the Post Office, and he fought with great flair during the War of Independence, when he was President of the Supreme Council of the IRA. However, with Arthur Griffith, Collins shared the responsibility for the 1921 Treaty which established the Irish Free State and accepted partition. He argued that the Treaty brought freedom and peace and could be viewed as a stepping-stone. There was considerable public support for this pragmatic approach, and Collins persuaded the Dail to accept the Treaty, in the face of bitter opposition from de Valera and resolute Republicans. Collins commanded the Free State forces during the ensuing Civil War. After the death of Griffith on 12 August 1922, Collins became Head of State and of the army, but he was killed in an IRA ambush twelve days later.

W. Hogan, c.1922. Developed out gelatine silver transparency.

James Quirke, said to be the last Republican to be
shot during the Civil War. The manner in which
his body is displayed and attended is all too
familiar from more recent scenes.
B. Leslie, Newcastlewest & Limerick, 1923. Gelatine
silver developed out print.

Alcock and Brown's aircraft crash-landed in
Derrygimla Bog, near Clifden, County Galway,
following their first non-stop transatlantic flight on
14-15 June 1919.
Unknown, 1919. Gelatine silver developed out print.

REVIVAL & REVOLUTION

First solo round-the-world flight. Captain
Kingsford-Smith departs from Portmarnock,
County Dublin.
Graphic, 1930. Gelatine silver print developing
out paper.

The annual ball of the Cork IRA Reserves in the
Yorkville Casino, New York.
Empire Photographers, 1931. Gelatine silver developed
out print.

CORK I.R.A. RESERVES
OCT. 3. 1931

above The Irish Grand Prix, Phoenix Park, Dublin, 19 July 1930. C.R. Whitcroft in the Riley is leading from A.H. Dovey in an Alfa Romeo. *Express Photos,* 1930. Gelatine silver print.

right Dr Pat O'Callaghan (1905-91), athlete. At the 1928 Games in Amsterdam, Pat O'Callaghan became the first citizen of the Irish Free State to win an Olympic Gold medal, in the hammer event. Four years later he won a second Olympic Gold, the only representative of his country to do so. He was still competing in 1936 but was unable to take part in the Games because of a dispute over whether athletes who were members of an All-Ireland association should be allowed to compete on behalf of the 26 counties of the Free State. *Central News,* Los Angeles, 1932. Gelatine silver developed out print.

REVIVAL & REVOLUTION

Rehousing the Claddagh. Between 1923 and 1931 almost 2,000 homes a year were built with state aid. It was a start, but given the poor conditions in which many Irish people were living it was woefully inadequate. Between 1932 and 1942 the government built an average of 12,000 homes annually.

Archief Exemplaar, Amsterdam, c.1930. Gelatine silver developed out print.

Numbers in italics refer to photographs

Abercorn, Lord *41*
Aberdeen, Lord and Lady *139*
Achill Island, Co. Mayo *90, 106, 107*
Alcock and Brown *198*
Anglo-Irish, the 115–17, *119*
Anglo-Irish Treaty (1921) 168, *195, 196*
Antrim, Co.: farm *108*
Aran Islands *96*
Aranmore *91*
army *see* British Army; Irish Army
Asquith, Herbert 11, 166
Atkins, Ringrose *155*
Ayton, A. *74*

Baldwin sisters *22*
Bandon Cricket Club *134*
Bandon family 67, 68, *127*
Banks, Robert 9, *80, 81, 85*
Bantry House *131*
Barrington, Sir Jonah 115
Belfast 137, 140, *148*;
    Albert Memorial *148*;
    Orangemen *146*, 165;
    steam tram *156*; *see
    also* Harland & Wolff
Berkeley, George 116
Bianconi, Charles *159*
Biggar, J. G. 163
Birr Castle 9
Black and Tans *183, 187, 189*
Blinkthorn, Captain *45*
Boland, Harry *195*
Boycott, Capt. Charles 175
British Army 9, 40, 45, *46, 48, 50*, 166, *183, 190, 191*
British Relief Association 40
Brugha, Cathal 168
Bullock Brothers *175*
Burke, Edmund 116
Burke, J. H. *171*
Burke, Thomas *175*

Cairo gang, the *187*
Carson, Edward 167, *180*

cartes de visite 14
'Cartes Siamoises' 14
Casement, Sir Roger 167
'Catholic Association' 36
Catholics *74*, 115, 165, 167, *172*; Emancipation 35, 36, 140
Cavehill and Whitewell Tramway *156*
Cavendish, Lord Frederick *175*
Chamberlain, Joseph 165
Chancellor *39, 182*
Charleton *48*
Chichester, Christine *96, 99, 101, 105, 110, 111, 113, 137, 144, 145*
Childers, Erskine 166
children *137, 137*, 139–40, *145*
Churchill, Lord Randolph 165
Civil War (1922–3) 11, *113, 164*, 168, *192, 193, 195, 197*
clachans 54, 56
Claddagh, Galway 11, *204*
Clare, Co.: *Leon XIII 98*; *see also* Vandeleur
Claremorris, Co. Mayo *159*
Clonbrock, Lady Augusta *see* Crofton, Augusta
Clonbrock, Luke Dillon, Lord *8, 116, 120*
Clonbrock House *8, 9, 116, 124*
Cloncurry, Lady *31*
Clonmacnoise, Co. Offaly *62*
Colleen Bawn Caves *64*
Collins, Michael 11, 168, *187, 195, 196*
Congested Districts Board 54
Connemara *39, 96*
Connolly, James 167, *182*
Cork, Co.: Bandon Cricket Club *134*; Castle Bernard *127*; Castletown-roche *70*; Castletownsend *94, 102*; Cork City *157*; Donemark *20*
Cosgrove, William *195*
country houses 7, 8, 115*ff*
Crace, John Gregory *13, 17, 22*
Crofton, Lady Augusta (and circle) *8, 9, 13, 22, 26, 70, 116, 120, 123, 124, 126, 128, 132*
Crofton family *8, 22*, 115, *120*
Curragh Mutiny 166
curraghs *93*

Currey, Francis Edmund *7, 8, 9, 14, 18, 21, 26, 29, 119*

daguerreotypes 7, 13
Dail, the 167, 168, *195, 196*
Darcy, Augustavus *26*
Davitt, Michael 11, *175*
de Valera, Eamon 11, 167, 168, *195, 196*
Devenish Island *61*
Devonshire, Duke of 7, 8, 17
Devoy, John 163
'diamond cameos' 14
Dickinson, Kate *95*
Dillon, John *175*
Dillon, Hon. Katie *115*
Dillon, Luke *see* Clonbrock, Lord
Disderi, André 9
Donaghy, James *172*
Donegal, Co. 9, *74, 80, 82*
'Donnybrooks' 56
Dovey, A. H. *202*
Down, Co. *108, 149*
Drogheda: The Quays *155*
Dublin: Balbriggan *189*; barracks *46, 190*; Docks and Customs House *42*; Mansion House *192*; O'Connell Bridge and St *141, 143, 182, 183*; Phoenix Park *202*; photographer's studios 13, 14; shop *138*; slums and tenements *137*, 137–9, *144, 145*; trams *143*; Trinity College 165; Vice-Regal Lodge *41*
Dublin Photographic Society 9, 10
Dungarvan Harbour, Co. Waterford *26*
Dunraven, Lord: *Notes on Irish Architecture 57, 61, 62*
Dyson, Colonel *39*

Easter Rising (1916) 7, 165, 167, 168, *181, 182, 195, 196*
Edgeworth, Maria 116
Edward VII *39*
Emmet, Robert 35, 167
Empire Photographers *200*
Erne, Lord *175*
evictions 9, 53, *76, 77, 78, 80, 82, 85, 86*, 163
Express Photos *202*

factories 137
fairs 56

Falcarragh, Co. Donegal: evictions 9, *80*
famines 7, 13, 38, 40, 53, 54, 116–17
farming 53, 54, *55, 56, 67, 68, 70, 101, 108, 112*, 117
Fenians 7, 11, *163, 163, 171, 172, 175*
festivals 56
Fianna Fail 11, *195*
fishing 53, 54, *93, 94, 96, 98, 99, 107*
Fitzgerald, Lord Otho *10, 31, 122*
French, Robert 14, *46, 57, 61, 62, 64, 82, 88, 90, 93, 106, 107, 131, 141, 148, 155, 157, 159, 171, 177*
funerals *110, 111*, 139–40, *189*

Gaelic League 165
Galway, Co.: Kilcornan *128*; Kilmacduach tower *62*; Leenane *88*; market *151*; relief works *92*; *see also* Clonbrock
George III 35
George IV 36
George V 166
Gillies, Mr 35
Gladstone, W. E. 10, 164, 165, 177
Goff, Tom *45*
Goldsmith, Oliver 116
Gonne, Maud *172*
Graphic *199*
Grattan, Henry 116
Graves, Rev. James *53*
Griffith, Arthur *139*, 168, *196*
Guinness family 139
Guy, Francis *78*

Haines, Humphrey *70*
Hallowe'en 56
Harland & Wolff shipyard 11, *151, 153*
Hartsook *195*
hawkers, Irish *103*
haymaking 68
Hemphill, Dr William *29*
Heraghty, Mary *87*
Hogan, W. *187, 196*
Home Rule 10, 37, 54, *146*, 165, 166–8, 177, 180
horse riders *135*; *see also* hunting
housing 11, *105, 204*; *see also* country houses
Humphries, Father *176*
hunting *119, 132*

Hyde, Douglas 165, *172*

Industrial Revolution 137
IRA *see* Irish Republican Army
IRB *see* Irish Republican Brotherhood
Irish Army 9, *164, 190*
Irish Free State 168, *195, 196, 202*
Irish Grand Prix *202*
Irish Nationalist Party 165–6, 167
Irish Party 163, *164*, 165, *177*
Irish People 163
Irish Republican Army 167, *187, 189, 192, 193, 195, 196, 200*
Irish Republican Brotherhood 163, 165, 167, 168, *171, 175, 181*
Irish Transport & General Workers' Union *182*
Irish Volunteers 165, 167
Irish Women's Workers' Union *182*

Jennings, Payne *24, 33, 42*
Johnston, Charles *151*
Joyce, James 165

Kells: Ancient Cross *57*
Kelly, Mary Eva *171*
Kenmare, Co. Kerry *159*
Kerry, Co.: funeral *110, 111*; railway *113*
Kickham, Charles 11, *163*
Kilburn, Mr *8*
Kildare, Co. 53; British Army *46, 48*
Kilkenny, Co. 53; mill worker *53*
Killarney: Colleen Bawn Caves *64*; Middle Lake *33*; Old Weir Bridge *24*
Kilmainham Treaty 165, 177
Kilronan Castle *129*
King, Gen. Robert *131*
King-Tenison, Edward *129*
Kingsford-Smith, Capt. *199*
Knock: open-air Mass *160*

Lafayette *132, 168*
Lamb, Captain *45*
Land Acts 53, 117, *164*–5
Land League 165, *175, 176, 177*
Land War (1879) 7
Larkin, Delia *182*
Larkin, James *182*